PREFACE

As a working woman you are challenged to excel in spite of the odds, which may range from inequities in the workplace to primary domestic responsibility to a workplace where change is the only guarantee.

The Woman Manager is written for and dedicated to those women who are in or aspire to management positions, who choose to assume increased responsibilities in their current positions whether in profit or nonprofit sectors, or who choose to start and grow their own businesses.

This book is especially dedicated to those women who have grown with me since my consciousness was raised and my commitment made in the late 1970s to help women move up and maximize opportunities in the workplace. To the thousands of women I've taught in college and university credit Women In Management courses, or trained in seminars or given speeches to in countless women's organizations—thank you.

The Woman Manager is a refinement of those courses, seminars, speeches to provide you with the practical, applicable concepts, techniques to become the woman manager you were meant to be.

Connie Sitterly

ABOUT THIS BOOK

THE WOMAN MANAGER is not like most books. It has a unique "self-paced" format that encourages a reader to become personally involved. Designed to be "read with a pencil," there are an abundance of exercises, activities, assessments and cases that invite participation.

This book is offered as a guide to taking a personal assessment and development journey to recognize your strengths, confirm your abilities, and enhance or develop those techniques and skills essential to all managers' success, but more profoundly for women's professional success.

The Woman Manager (and the other self-improvement books listed in the back of this book) can be used effectively a number of ways. Here are some possibilities:

► **Individual Study.** Because the book is self-instructional, all that is needed is a quiet place, some time and a pencil. Completing the activities and exercises should provide not only valuable feedback, but also practical ideas about improving your managerial skills.

► **Workshops and Seminars.** The book is ideal for preassigned reading prior to a workshop or seminar. With the basics in hand, the quality of participation should improve. More time can be spent on concept extensions and applications during the program. The book is also effective when distributed at the beginning of a session.

► **Remote Location Training.** Copies can be sent to those not able to attend "home office" training sessions.

► **Informal Study Groups.** Thanks to the format, brevity and low cost, this book is ideal for "brown-bag" or other informal group sessions.

There are other possibilities that depend on the objectives of the user. One thing is for sure: even after it has been read, this book will serve as excellent reference material that can be easily reviewed. Good luck!

THE WOMAN MANAGER
Developing Essential Skills for Success

Connie Sitterly, Ed.D.

A FIFTY-MINUTE™ SERIES BOOK

CRISP PUBLICATIONS, INC.
Menlo Park, California

THE WOMAN MANAGER
Developing Essential Skills for Success

Connie Sitterly, Ed.D.

CREDITS:
Editor: **Bev Manber**
Typesetting: **ExecuStaff**
Cover Design: **Carol Harris**
Artwork: **Ralph Mapson**

Copyright © 1993 Connie Sitterly, Ed.D. CPCM
Printed in the United States of America by Bawden Printing Company.

English language Crisp books are distributed worldwide. Our major international distributors include:

CANADA: Reid Publishing, Ltd., Box 69559—109 Thomas St., Oakville, Ontario Canada L6J 7R4. TEL: (416) 842-4428; FAX: (416) 842-9327

AUSTRALIA: Career Builders, P.O. Box 1051, Springwood, Brisbane, Queensland, Australia 4127. TEL: 841-1061, FAX: 841-1580

NEW ZEALAND: Career Builders, P.O. Box 571, Manurewa, Auckland, New Zealand. TEL: 266-5276, FAX: 266-4152

JAPAN: Phoenix Associates Co., Mizuho Bldg. 2-12-2, Kami Osaki, Shinagawa-Ku, Tokyo 141, Japan. TEL: 3-443-7231, FAX: 3-443-7640

Selected Crisp titles are also available in other languages. Contact International Rights Manager Tim Polk at (800) 442-7477 for more information.

Library of Congress Catalog Card Number 92-075717
Sitterly, Connie
The Woman Manager
ISBN 1-56052-206-2

This book is printed on recyclable paper with soy ink.

ABOUT THE AUTHOR

Dr. Connie Sitterly, CPCM (Ed.D.), owner and founder of Management Training Specialists (MTS), is an award-winning international speaker, trainer, and consultant for both public and private sectors.

Dr. Sitterly has received numerous awards, including:

- Who's Who in Finance & Industry

- Who's Who in Education

- International Customer Service Award—Outstanding Commitment to Customer Service

- Top Professor Award, Texas Woman's University Mortar Board

- American Society of Training & Development Award—Practical Application Award

Dr. Sitterly is the author of five management texts, more than two hundred magazine and newspaper articles, and a six-tape cassette series.

Dr. Sitterly is a frequent radio and TV show guest and an adjunct professor in the Department of Business & Economics at Texas Woman's University in Denton, Texas. She is a frequent speaker at international, national and state conferences and is a certified professional consultant to management.

For more information on Dr. Connie Sitterly, call or write to:

Management Training Specialists
550 Bailey, Suite 210
Fort Worth, TX 76107
(817) 332-3612 - Fax (817) 338-0737

CONTENTS

INTRODUCTION: WHAT IT TAKES 1

PART I: WOMEN IN MANAGEMENT 7
    Leadership: ''You've Come a Long Way, Baby'' 9
    Setting and Achieving Goals 22
    Moving Up 28

PART II: ESSENTIAL MANAGEMENT SKILLS 37
    Time Management 39
    Communicating for Results 52
    Negotiation 63
    Making Decisions and Solving Problems 67

PART III: GET ON TOP AND STAY THERE 75
    Understanding Power and Politics 77
    Managing Stress 83

APPENDIXES 91
    Appendix A: Managers' Needs Inventory Review 93
    Appendix B: Glossary 95
    Appendix C: Suggested Readings/Resources .98

INTRODUCTION: WHAT IT TAKES

> *"Take risks. You can't fall off the bottom."*
> Barbara Proctor (1933–   )
> American Advertising Executive

In *Megatrends 2000: Ten New Directions for the 1990s,* authors John Naisbitt and Patricia Aburdene say, "To be a leader in business today, it is no longer an advantage to have been socialized as male."

Although there has never been a better time for women to move into management, author Fannie Hurst's remark that "A woman has to be twice as good as a man to go half as far," still holds merit. For example, in 1985, only 2 percent, or 29 of 1,362 senior corporate executives surveyed by Korn/Ferry International were women.

We want it all—job, raises, promotions, perks, training, visibility—and we are willing to do whatever it takes to get ahead.

For those women who aspire to management, it takes more than skills such as time management, delegation, problem solving, negotiation and assertiveness. It takes commitment, leadership and the ability to set and achieve goals and take risks.

The 1990s have been named the "decade of/for women"—what businesses need now are the values that women have been socialized to provide. Women's values of caring, intuition and consideration for the world as a whole are transforming organizations. Changes in values, technology, labor availability, the workforce, lifestyles, public attitudes, family roles, globalization, legal requirements, company reorganization, emphasis on teamwork and employee involvement are all factors that will enhance women's opportunities to compete and survive in tough economic times.

In spite of the trend to eliminate mid-management level positions, the Bureau of Labor Statistics's list of occupations revealed that general managers and top executives ranked sixth as the occupations that will offer the most new jobs. The Bureau also projects that between the years 1990 and 2005, the United States will need 600,000 new managers and top executives.

INTRODUCTION: WHAT IT TAKES
(continued)

Since conditioning has reinforced women to wait to be asked to get married and to be asked out on a date, waiting to be asked to consider a promotion or leadership position may too often or too easily follow. Assuming that superior performance will be recognized and rewarded, how long can you afford to wait to share ambitions, strengths and accomplishments, in terms of how they will benefit your employer?

Review the Attributes of Managers

Commit—Do whatever it takes within legal and ethical limits to fulfill promises and requirements in the most courteous, responsive, reliable, error-free manner, on time, every time.

Lead—Get involved at work by *volunteering* to lead; participate on a team or committee at work or in a professional organization.

Set Goals—Set and share goals with those who can help you attain them. Do not wait for people to read your mind about what you want or need. Share what you want, why you want it, what you have done, what you are currently doing, and what you are going to do. Communicate need for support or assistance.

Take Risks—Take risks, make decisions and suggestions, volunteer for projects and teams, and empower yourself to take action.

Persevere—Sticking with a course of action can be tough. Realize that learning to take criticism is part of any job. Do not give up until you reach your goal.

Project a Positive Image—Because first impressions can often be lasting impressions, it is important to project not only an image of competence and pride, but one that positively reflects on the company and its leadership.

Gain visibility and support by demonstrating unquestionable ethics, a participating style, and a professional image at all times.

Women are more likely than men to be criticized for a poor image, mannerisms, speech patterns, gestures and posture. The questions they ask, and their sense of humor, or lack of it, not only influence the image they present, but are critical to business success. Right or wrong, fair or unfair, studies show that women are judged more on their style than substance, giving new meaning to the perennial question, ''What will I wear?''

As Betty Haragan, author of *Games Mother Never Taught You,* says, ''There is no question in my mind that many women are held back in their job progress because of their inattention to dress. . . . Your clothes must convey that you are competent, self-confident, reliable and authoritative.''

Learn Continuously—Be open to new sources of help or information. Take advantage of your company's education tuition and fee-reimbursement programs, take courses at your own expense, utilize company resources and training programs. Consider reading other Crisp *50-MINUTE* books on specific topics, listed in the back of this book.

Be Optimistic—Keep a positive attitude about your career. Visualize your success. View obstacles as opportunities to make a difference by making suggestions or taking action.

Learning the behind-the-scenes politics or operations of a job takes time. Companies feel more comfortable promoting someone they have seen perform reliably and competently over a period of time.

INTRODUCTION: WHAT IT TAKES
(continued)

Develop Positioning Strategies

Which of these strategies are applicable to you or your situation?

- Attend corporate and community social and project meetings.

- Document individual or group results or achievements or your department or project team, and submit them to your company newsletter or newspaper.

- Volunteer for presentations within and outside your company.

- Seek high-visibility projects, first-time positions, or new change-oriented issues with which to associate and dedicate time and effort.

Accept Changing Values

Mothers with preschool-age children are the fastest growing segment of the labor force. Over 60 percent of all families are now represented in the labor force by mothers with responsibility for over ten million children under the age of six. Recent studies show that work affects marriage and children less than marriage and children affect a woman's career progress.

A prime example is demonstrated by the movie, *Baby Boom.* Diane Keaton portrayed a successful, mobile, career woman whose upward progress in the company comes to a halt when she inherits her cousin's toddler. An older, married man in the company advises her that he had to make a choice long ago between career and family, that he never saw his kids growing up and does not know them. The implied threat in his words is that she, as a woman executive, cannot have a ''family'' life and continue to be an asset to the company.

The prevailing attitude in business has been an either/or choice that disallowed successful males from enjoying a well-rounded life that balanced career and family. Successful males in business sacrificed personal attachments for money and strategic positions. Women in business labored in jobs of servitude to upwardly mobile males.

In the past twenty years, the United States economy and the women's movement have forced business to include women in career tracks formerly closed to them. Yet, myths still prevail, such as women will leave work to attend to a sick child, and women cannot be promoted to a prestigious job that requires relocation, because a husband's job takes priority.

Women can and will become the primary driving force to sensitize American organizations in which they are employed to incorporate the changing needs of today's workforce. Increasingly, businesses are recognizing some of the special needs of women with families and careers.

New employment practices have been adopted to accommodate these needs. Some of these practices are:

✔ **Flextime**—Some companies may allow employees, with prior approval, to alter their working hours.

✔ **Permanent part-time**—Some companies allow employees to work a part-time schedule for permanent part-time benefits.

✔ **Job sharing**—In some companies, two employees share one full-time position by splitting responsibilities into two part-time jobs.

✔ **Flexplace**—Some employees are allowed to work at home, rather than in an office or plant.

✔ **Compressed work week**—Some employers are shortening the work week, so that the number of hours per day increases, and the number of days decreases, such as a 4-day, 40-hour week, saving overhead costs and providing employees with a three-day weekend on a regular basis.

Move Up or Move On?

Allow employers a chance to modify or create opportunities for you before you make the decision to move on. If you think it is time to find another job, discuss your perceptions, concerns and desires with your manager and/or personnel manager. If you leave without discussing possible changes, you may unnecessarily short-change yourself, your manager and your company.

If you dread going to work in the morning, are bored or lack a challenge in your work, or if activities are no longer interesting and meaningful, it may be time to change or move on. Other indicators might be completing tasks you do not like, want to do, or do poorly, believing you are not fairly compensated for your efforts, having insufficient opportunities for development and independence, or having an unresolved personality conflict with your manager, another associate or your team leader.

INTRODUCTION: WHAT IT TAKES
(continued)

If you receive indications that women in general, or you in particular, have few opportunities for promotion within the corporation and you continue to be overlooked for promotions, even after you have made your desires known, it is definitely time to move on.

There is no one career path. Team leaders or managers can come from any area of an organization. You will likely be successful to the degree you believe in and enjoy what you do.

Consider both long and short-term career goals. Taking a horizontal transfer to a position with no greater responsibility to learn more about other functions or products, or taking an entry-level job to gain experience with the right company may be short-term sacrifices to achieve long-term goals.

Despite numerous obstacles and unfavorable conditions facing women in the business world today, many corporations are taking action to increase opportunities for women within their organizations. It is important, meanwhile, for each woman to know her rights and to know what action can be taken to enforce those rights. The slogan, ''You've come a long way baby,'' is correct, but we still have a long way to go.

P   A   R   T

I

Women in Management

- Leadership: "You've Come a Long Way, Baby"
- Setting and Achieving Goals
- Moving Up

LEADERSHIP: "YOU'VE COME A LONG WAY, BABY"

> *"It is better to be a lion for a day than a sheep all your life."*
> Sister Elizabeth Kenny (1886–1952)
> Australian Nurse

In the 1970s, Virginia Slims gave us a slogan that is a reminder of how far we have come. But how much farther do we have to go? What challenges do we still face?

While management's objective to utilize people and resources effectively to achieve the organization's goals has remained unchanged, the approaches, styles and techniques of management continue to change. Today's woman manager must possess superior people skills to effectively:

✔ Delegate and empower

✔ Solve problems innovatively, through consensus decision-making

✔ Articulate the vision, values, philosophy and goals

✔ Foster teamwork in the spirit of cooperation and collaboration

Factors Holding Women Back

► **Lack of Role Models**—It may be the *Decade of Women*, but today, still, fewer than 5 percent of top managers are women.

► **Lack of Equal Pay**—In 1993, a woman earns about 74 cents for every dollar a man brings home. This is an increase of about nine cents in a decade, even though women are better educated and hold more highly skilled positions than ten years ago.

LEADERSHIP: "YOU'VE COME A LONG WAY BABY" (continued)

► **Discrimination**—People who hire people like themselves tend to trust their performance record to meeting certain standards, blocking others from management/leadership opportunities. For example, men who hire and promote primarily men, due to such a vested interest or status-quo mentality, impede women's progress regardless of their potential contribution to the organizations. According to a recent poll conducted by *Fortune* magazine, of 201 chief executives of the nation's largest companies, only 16 percent feel it is *very likely* that they could be succeeded by a female CEO in the next decade. Of the several reasons listed, discrimination is seen as the biggest barrier.

► **Feelings of Isolation**—Isolation is common among nontraditional women, and women in management positions. Often they may be the only woman in a roomful of males and have no female counterparts.

► **Statistical Time Lag Between Entry-Level Jobs and Management**—This typically takes 15 to 20 years, but throughout this decade we will see increasing numbers of women penetrate top positions in every profession.

► **Stereotypes**—Treating women as mother, daughter, wife or girlfriend, or categorizing and believing that women are emotional, bitchy or picky is stereotypical. It also undermines relationships and results. Equally detrimental are women who react to men as if they are fathers, brothers, husbands, or boyfriends, assuming that they are unemotional, even-tempered, and inherently can repair and lift any item.

► **Glass Ceiling Effect**—The "Glass Ceiling Effect," coined by Ann Morrison, author of *Breaking Through the Glass Ceiling*, refers to a transparent barrier or subtle discrimination against women's mobility. The "Glass Ceiling" impedes women from moving up to senior management *because they are women*. Many women reach the glass ceiling and, once this level has been met, become frustrated at the lack of promotional opportunities. It is at this point that many women decide to venture into their own businesses.

For every problem listed there are solutions. For some women, it is starting their own business; for others it may be learning some lessons from male colleagues. Men learned to focus on winning, valuing independence and competition in team sports, in the military, and in college under the tutelage of male mentors. Our tendency as women is to focus on collaboration for long-term interaction.

THE FEMALE ENTREPRENEUR

Currently, 70 percent of all businesses are being started by women who are willing to tie their rewards directly to their own efforts. When advancement opportunities seem too slow, they take the risks necessary to drive their dreams to reality.

Note the Following:

- Over five million women-owned businesses generate more jobs than the Fortune 500 companies.

- Women-owned businesses are among the fastest-growing segments of the U.S. economy.

- Between 40 and 50 percent of businesses will be owned by women by the year 2010.

In increasing numbers, disillusioned women are leaving corporations to start their own businesses. These women are leaving corporations without the needed pool of talent and performance.

Why are the track records so startling for women entrepreneurs? In *Megatrends for Women,* Janet Harris-Lange, president of the National Association of Women Business Owners, states that women business owners are more likely to succeed than men, because women admit they need help and surround themselves with good people. Beatrice Fitzpatrick, founder and president of the American Women's Economic Development Corporation, states that, ''A woman would no more let her business fail than she would let someone kill her child.''

The Female Entrepreneur by Dr. Sitterly, also published by Crisp Publications, Inc., includes more information on the challenges the woman entrepreneur faces. It identifies strategies to start and succeed in your own business.

THE FEMALE ENTREPRENEUR (continued)

You can expect that between the years 2000 to 2010, 40 to 50 percent of all businesses will be owned by women. These businesses will have an admirable success rate—75 percent of women-owned businesses succeed, compared with twenty percent of total businesses. Considering that over 40 percent of women-owned businesses have gross sales of $250,000, and over 15 percent have gross sales of over $1,000,000, it is time to acknowledge, if not celebrate, the veritable force and contribution of women-owned businesses.

Are You Ready to Take the Risk?

If you are thinking of starting your own business, ask yourself, ''Do I have'':

- ☐ Sufficient capitalization for two years

- ☐ A workable business plan

- ☐ Family support

- ☐ Willingness to trade security for the risk of a new adventure

- ☐ Willingness to reinvest profits back into the business

- ☐ The discipline to sustain both personal and professional life

THREE AREAS OF SKILLS

The three basic areas of skills essential to become more effective in your current position or to move into management are technical, interpersonal and conceptual skills. Even though technical skills are likely the primary area of skills currently utilized, develop interpersonal and conceptual skills now to facilitate the transition to higher positions, grade levels, or responsibilities as defined next.

1. TECHNICAL SKILLS

Mastering the tools, jargon and unique abilities characteristic of a given profession or job, are no longer sufficient to either ensure getting a job or being promoted.

2. INTERPERSONAL SKILLS

This refers to the ability to work effectively as a group/team member, in a spirit of collaboration, courtesy and cooperation, respecting the diverse needs and background of other people to achieve common goals.

Possessing superior people or interpersonal skills is essential to being effective in your current job or to being considered for leadership roles. Interpersonal skills are essential to build customer relationships by listening and responding to their needs. This benefits the company, fulfills job requirements, and ultimately enhances opportunities and job satisfaction.

3. CONCEPTUAL SKILLS

This is the ability to see the organization as a whole, to see how parts of the organization are interdependent on each other, or how changes in one area will affect another. It includes the ability to coordinate and interpret ideas, concepts and practices, and to analyze, forecast and plan—seeing the *big picture.*

THREE AREAS OF SKILLS (continued)

Managers or ''team leaders'' translate plans and policies into objectives. They:

- Review and evaluate employees and team members

- Serve as spokespersons between managers and team members

- Implement projects

- Organize and direct tasks

- Train and cross-train employees

- Enforce procedures and policies

The trend today, as companies downsize, restructure and form teams is to reduce mid-level management. It is crucial to career success to volunteer for team responsibilities, develop team skills necessary to facilitate and participate on teams, and to welcome such changes.

Top managers—renamed ''coaches'' in some companies:

- Develop and implement business plans and strategies

- Conceptualize data and plot the company's future

- Inspire by example, and articulate the vision

- Address strategic issues such as:

    ► quality

    ► service

    ► empowerment

    ► teamwork

    ► diversity

MANAGEMENT FUNCTIONS

Men and women may differ in styles, approaches or attributes. Regardless, mastering the basic functions of management—planning, organizing, staffing and controlling—are essential to men and women becoming effective managers or team leaders.

Management Functions Quick Check

Place a "+" beside each of the following functions that are your strongest. Place a "✓" beside those that need the most development.

☐ **Plan.** Decide who, what, when, where, why and how things will be done, in view of the organization's goals and the team's capabilities; develop and interpret policies; manage budgets and continuously improve methods of performing specific tasks.

☐ **Organize.** Prepare schedules, delegate tasks and monitor progress through timetables or measurable objectives.

☐ **Staff.** Advise and support associates, recommend qualified team members for hire and promotion; evaluate individual and group performance; develop and reward associates.

☐ **Direct.** Motivate, inspire and communicate with associates for better understanding, ownership and commitment; seek to reduce response or process time by encouraging innovation.

☐ **Control.** Measure performance, establish standards and measurements of quality and service, prevent and correct problems that impede effectiveness, and obtain feedback for current and future projects.

What particular tasks or projects can help you develop these abilities? To expedite the process, consider setting relevant goals and sharing your desire to develop one or more of these areas with your manager, team leader or training/human resource manager.

EXERCISE: LEADERSHIP QUALITIES OF THE WOMAN MANAGER

As a successful woman manager, you must possess essential leadership qualities and attitudes to achieve objectives, bring about decisions, solve problems, reduce waste, cut costs, generate profits and set standards.

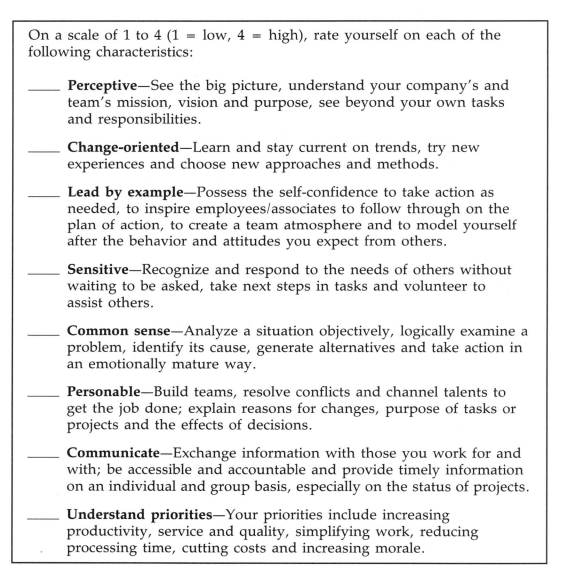

On a scale of 1 to 4 (1 = low, 4 = high), rate yourself on each of the following characteristics:

_____ **Perceptive**—See the big picture, understand your company's and team's mission, vision and purpose, see beyond your own tasks and responsibilities.

_____ **Change-oriented**—Learn and stay current on trends, try new experiences and choose new approaches and methods.

_____ **Lead by example**—Possess the self-confidence to take action as needed, to inspire employees/associates to follow through on the plan of action, to create a team atmosphere and to model yourself after the behavior and attitudes you expect from others.

_____ **Sensitive**—Recognize and respond to the needs of others without waiting to be asked, take next steps in tasks and volunteer to assist others.

_____ **Common sense**—Analyze a situation objectively, logically examine a problem, identify its cause, generate alternatives and take action in an emotionally mature way.

_____ **Personable**—Build teams, resolve conflicts and channel talents to get the job done; explain reasons for changes, purpose of tasks or projects and the effects of decisions.

_____ **Communicate**—Exchange information with those you work for and with; be accessible and accountable and provide timely information on an individual and group basis, especially on the status of projects.

_____ **Understand priorities**—Your priorities include increasing productivity, service and quality, simplifying work, reducing processing time, cutting costs and increasing morale.

On those items you rated less than 3, identify ways to improve. Discuss them with your manager within the next seven days.

Process Teams

Participating or leading a process team is valuable for any woman who aspires to move up in an organization. It provides new skills, visibility, contacts and training.

No one person has the solution for all problems in business. Women's "feminine management style," by nature of being nurturing, open and sensitive to others' feelings and needs, lends itself especially well to the 1990s team approach of participative or consensus decision-making. Japanese cultural workplace values are one reason for their explosive success. For example, they place the good of their team and/or entire company above their individual needs. Consequently, the Japanese have eclipsed many American companies as leaders in new product development and production by forming groups of two or more persons, called process teams. Sometimes called "Quality Circles" in the United States, they are gaining increasing popularity in American companies, to improve methods and increase productivity. They have been successful in lowering resistance, improving satisfaction, communication and innovation.

Participation is usually voluntary. It is characterized by short meetings that have the approval and commitment of management. Commitment is demonstrated by being open to the team's ideas, as well as good faith effort toward implementation of the workable ideas. Without this commitment, the employees would resent time given to meetings from which there would be no results.

Members and leaders are trained fully to involve and solicit ideas from fellow team members and avoid meetings characterized by peripheral problems or personal feelings. The team identifies problems and evaluates alternatives, proposes recommendations, and weighs the solutions against cost and time effectiveness.

The woman manager/team leader must ensure that numerous responsibilities, projects and tasks are accomplished on or before time through the collaborative efforts of team building. Her work must be completed within or under budget; it must be error free and meet or exceed standards of quality, service and production.

To maximize your career opportunities, develop teamwork skills by volunteering to be on an existing team or starting a new team to address a specific situation requiring improvement. With the trend toward downsizing, reorganization and elimination of layers of management, opportunities lie in assuming team leadership roles.

Responsibilities Quick Check

Place a "✓" by the responsibilities you believe you should develop further.
Place a "+" beside the ones you feel are already your strong abilities.

☐ Administer resources; evaluate and schedule funds, equipment, training, supplies, time and staff.

☐ Solicit suggestions and recommendations, recognize and encourage associates; implement ideas, giving credit to individuals and/or teams.

☐ Assist associates with organizing and prioritizing their individual work to meet team objectives and to do whatever it takes to complete the job, thereby regardless of preset job descriptions.

☐ Lead and empower employees; encourage associates to follow through on the job, thereby inspiring initiative, trust, ownership and commitment to deliver the most responsive, professional service possible.

☐ Continuously develop and train; provide adequate instructions in delegating assignments; continuously train and cross-train, in both technical and professional development skills. Earn trust by giving trust, respect and accountability; demonstrate your confidence in the team, allow for mistakes or setbacks, and recognize and reward those who contribute ideas or participate in change.

☐ Involve in a decision those who will be affected by or contribute to its implementation; unless it is a black and white authority-based decision, consult or involve those who will carry out or be affected by the decision in the planning stage, even if they are in another department, area, or on another team.

☐ Develop your sense of humor. Lighten up! Having fun and enjoying work is an expectation of increasingly more employees today.

☐ Avoid an *us-against-them* approach to team building. After all, every team, area and department is dependent on every other team, area and department to fulfill their common goals. They should respect the requests and needs of associates as their own.

To develop those abilities that you have noted above, share them with your manager or a coworker. Compare perceptions, solutions and resources; develop an action plan.

HINTS FOR RELATIONSHIP DEVELOPMENT WITH YOUR MANAGER

Develop a cordial, yet professional, relationship with your manager. A business relationship may be too close for comfort. Being viewed as an inseparable pair can be detrimental to your image and reputation.

► Treat your manager as you want to be treated. Respect your boss's time, prepare for discussions, follow through on requests, provide updates on projects and take next-step initiative.

► Help your boss reach his or her stated objectives. If your manager's goal is to improve quality, what can you do to improve quality? If you do not know what your manager's goals are, ask.

► Think positively! Identify and share what is good about your manager, the department and the company. Be a part of the solution, not the problem; share situations and their impact, and propose solutions, including the action that you are personally willing to take to correct or improve the situation.

► Do not gossip. Gossip can not only sabotage a career, it can destroy the morale of an entire department or company. People who leak information or talk carelessly about other people in an office will not be trusted, and will likely be bypassed for leadership opportunities. Keep confidential information private.

► Keep your boss informed of your accomplishments, both on and off the job—such as completing a course, graduating or earning a certification. When appropriate, share the credit with others responsible for the success.

► Monkey see, monkey do: learn the unwritten rules of the company. By developing the work habits and values of top managers, you may be considered *management material*.

► Empower. Demonstrate confidence in associates by giving them the commensurate authority and allowing enough room for them to try their own ideas and methods.

► Promise only what you can deliver and deliver what you promise. To retain credibility, follow through on requests, even if it means carrying around a promise pad to record specifically to whom, what and when action is expected. Then, meet or exceed expectations.

HINTS FOR RELATIONSHIP DEVELOPMENT WITH YOUR MANAGER (continued)

► Listen more than you speak. Listening shows you respect their ideas and their right to express them, and lets you know what motivates that individual. In most instances, listen 80 percent of the time, and speak 20 percent of the time. Notice your response or reaction to those who listen 20 percent of the time and speak 80 percent. Make notes, summarize and paraphrase to ensure understanding.

► Recognize and reward. A certificate or plaque, mention in the company newsletter, an E-mail message on the computer, a specialty item like a jacket, mug or pen with the corporate logo, a bonus check, dinner for two, or movie tickets that says "thanks," "good job," "I appreciate your effort," will be remembered. People do what gets rewarded and support those who recognize their best efforts.

Opportunities for recognition include:

- Achieving a production goal, sales quota or perfect attendance

- Submitting a suggestion

- Participating in community service work or a civic project

- Receiving a commendation from a customer for good service

- Completing a training program or business course

What are some opportunities to recognize others in your company, department or team not listed here?

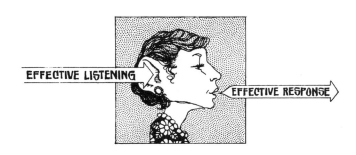

EXERCISE: YOUR RELATIONSHIP WITH YOUR MANAGER

To improve your relationship with your manager, make note of certain preferences and concerns. Answer the following questions about your manager.

1. What are the goals and mission that your boss is trying to accomplish? _____
   _____

2. What are some habits of employees/associates that usually irritate your boss? _____
   _____

3. How does your boss accept compliments? _____
   _____

4. What is the number one problem and priority facing your boss? ____
   _____

5. What are key personal facts, such as interests, hobbies, birthday and pet projects about your boss? _____
   _____

6. What does your boss regard as good performance—what gets rewarded? _____
   _____

7. What style of office politics does your boss practice? _____
   _____

8. What mood swings characterize your boss—when is the best and worst time for discussions? _____
   _____

9. How does your manager's management style differ from your style? _____
   _____

Know what is expected and how well you are doing; do jobs that others cannot or will not do; gain organization support; and develop good relationships with your managers or associates. While there are no guarantees, such advice will help to propel you to success in any organization.

SETTING AND ACHIEVING GOALS

> *"The future belongs to those who believe in the beauty of their dreams."*
>
> Eleanor Roosevelt (1884–1962)
> Humanitarian and writer, wife of President Franklin Delano Roosevelt.

With all the economic ups and downs in America today, your company could be sold or could buy another company. Change is a necessary and permanent factor in business. Your job is not going to remain static. No business will survive if it does not change to meet challenges such as growing competition, globalization, and a repressed economy.

Consequently, to manage such changes, it is essential to set and achieve clearly defined goals whether you choose to keep and enjoy your current position or climb the corporate ladder. The only guarantee is change; nothing remains the same. A cherished boss may be replaced. The company may be reorganized; massive layoffs may occur; and offices or plants may close, requiring relocation, demotion, or retraining. Women, especially, must develop insight into themselves and what we want, an idea that is keyed around setting realistic goals.

Reassessing what we want may be a lifetime process; goal-setting can speed up the process. Often, the difference between setting and not setting goals is the difference between working smart and working hard. We sometimes resist setting goals because it may be perceived as a time consuming, futile exercise. However, without them, we have no direction, no destination. Here are some tips on how to set and achieve goals.

Goals should be:

- **Realistic,** challenging, requiring improvement

- **Written**—start with an action verb such as "develop," "decrease," "reduce" or "save"

- **Specific**—use clear and concise language to communicate

- **Measurable**—defined by specific results and target dates

- Both **qualitative** and **quantitative,** whenever possible

- **Concurrent with your needs and values,** and preferably in concert with company and departmental goals

EXERCISE: ACCELERATE YOUR GOAL SETTING

Answer the following questions to help accelerate your goal-setting process:

1. What two or three results will make the greatest difference? What do you *really* want?

   _____

   _____

2. Do your goals support your primary needs?

   _____

   _____

3. How will achieving each goal specifically benefit you?

   _____

   _____

4. What are some of the obstacles you anticipate? What resources and support will you need to overcome them?

   _____

   _____

5. Who will you share your goals with, who will be able to encourage and assist you? Have you discussed your goals with your manager and those who can assist or support your efforts, personally and professionally? If not, why not and when will you discuss them?

   _____

   _____

6. How will you reward yourself when you achieve your goals?

   _____

   _____

ACHIEVEMENT BY OBJECTIVE

The most important question to ask and keep asking is: What have I done today toward the achievement of my goals? Goals are achieved in short "chunks" or sprints, and you need to keep that focus until you achieve them. One task, even as simple as making a key phone call or pulling a file, makes a difference.

Use the following worksheet as a guide as you record three specific goals you would like to achieve in three months, in six months, in a year, and in five years.

Goal-Setting Worksheet

Be specific: 3 months — 6 months — 1 year — 5 years

Professional

1. _____

2. _____

3. _____

Personal

1. _____

2. _____

3. _____

Financial (salary, earnings, investments, possessions)

1. _____

2. _____

3. _____

Physical

1. _____

2. _____

3. _____

Educational

1. _____
2. _____
3. _____

Social (trip, hobby, see a friend)

1. _____
2. _____
3. _____

To achieve these goals, outline what tasks must be achieved by breaking what may seem an overwhelming goal into achievable tasks. You may wish to use one outline for each goal identifying the tasks for today, those to be done this week, and those to be done this month.

WHAT WILL MAKE THE DIFFERENCE?

Identify two activities that will make the difference in each of the following categories. Be specific and add a target date.

CAREER

1. _____

2. _____

COMPANY

1. _____

2. _____

DEPARTMENT

1. _____

2. _____

BOSS

1. _____

2. _____

To design a well-balanced, fulfilling life, set specific goals with target dates, in the general areas of your life—social, physical, educational, professional and financial. From your list, determine one or two activities you will do daily to propel you toward your goal. Assign it a high priority. Make weekly, monthly and yearly goals **TODAY.**

EXERCISE: TRACKING GOAL ACHIEVEMENT

The exercise that follows has been provided to help you set your goals. A few examples of questions you should address are listed, with a chart to document your weekly, monthly and yearly goals.

What training/courses will I enroll in next? _____

_____

How can I increase my visibility and/or recognition in my organization?

_____

_____

What new task or responsibility can I seek within the next three months?

_____

_____

My Goals

	Week	Month	Year	Target Date
Professional				
Personal				
Financial				
Physical				
Educational				
Social				

Success is less what you have than what you make of it. You can make more of it—whatever *it* is—through setting and achieving goals, knowing what you enjoy, what you are best at, what gives you the greatest sense of reward and accomplishment, what feeds your pride, passion and persistence. The process of achieving your goals can be more meaningful than the results you achieve.

MOVING UP

> *"The person who knows how will always have a job.*
> *The person who knows why will always be his boss."*
>
> Diane Ravitch (1938–   )
> American educator

Women tapped for management usually possess more than desire and determination. Many also have the image, attitude, performance and people skills necessary to fill the position. To ensure a smooth transition from doer to delegator, the new manager or team leader must improve existing, or develop new abilities.

Strength Assessment Quick Check

To determine which area and specific ways you should focus on developing, place a "✓" in the box beside each item you feel you should strengthen as you prepare for the next challenge or position. Place a "+" beside each item that you believe is a strength you already possess.

☐ Bring about solutions to correct and prevent problems, by consulting with those affected by and contributing to the solution.

☐ Network with other supervisor/team leaders or business owners who are knowledgeable about company policies or unwritten rules.

☐ Give and welcome criticism, by recognizing a situation and being willing to discuss it objectively and propose solutions on how to improve, correct and prevent recurrence.

☐ Schedule time with each employee to find out what he or she perceives as the strengths and weaknesses of the department or team, and to discover special strengths, ambitions and concerns.

Transition Tips

TIP #1: Can you trade being liked for being respected? Not all your decisions will be popular decisions, and not everyone will like you. For many women, this can be difficult, because most women are socialized to believe that being liked or popular is essential.

TIP #2: People need to trust you, before they can trust your ideas. If you are contemplating changes, consult with key employees to gain their ideas on implementation, or consider how the change will affect them.

TIP #3: While it may be temporarily embarrassing to admit that you or your team made an error, it is best to admit the error and share how it can be corrected and prevented from occurring again. Blaming or covering up a mistake can have greater repercussions than the actual mistake. How you handle the situation may be more important than the situation.

MOVING UP (continued)

Bypassing

Bypassing means selecting alternate career path choices to overcome career barriers that keep you from moving ahead. Identify people who can provide the resources and information to assist you in your objectives, and go directly to them, regardless of their title or position.

Identify potential career barriers for new managers by answering "yes" or "no" to the following questions:

	Yes	No
1. Do you take criticism personally, rather than learning from your mistakes?	☐	☐
2. Do you have an all or nothing attitude—right or wrong, good or bad?	☐	☐
3. Do you focus on self-development and self-promotion, more than being part of a winning team, which makes everyone look good?	☐	☐
4. Do you capitulate to others' wishes without making your own thoughts known?	☐	☐
5. Do you fail to take risks that could ultimately benefit your career?	☐	☐
6. Do you fear success or failure?	☐	☐
7. Do you procrastinate on commitment and follow-through, including going back to school, sharing ambitions with manager, or joining a women's professional organization?	☐	☐

Review any questions you answered "yes" to above. What steps can you take to overcome these barriers?

Networking

Politicians know that contacts are their most important tools for reelection. They know how to wheel and deal to achieve their goals. So, too, do successful businessmen. No one works in a vacuum. Men hang out with each other and learn where the jobs are. They are not shy about meeting others who can influence their success. Young men seek mentors who can teach them and give them a boost. In today's world, knowing your particular business is not enough. One fallacy that many young women believe is that their talent *alone* will garner them promotions.

Women in business cannot succeed by being excellent in their jobs alone. Women should view contacts as windows on their world, and be prepared to reciprocate. Would you help a friend or acquaintance if that person were to ask you about job openings in your company? Would you write a recommendation to help someone get a job or promotion if you liked or respected that person?

Networking means using personal contacts to achieve a goal, get information, meet a key contact, or gain access to resources. Networking occurs when you ask people where they leased their copiers or who is a good speaker or trainer, or tell an associate about a job opening. Networking takes the power derived from positioning and links it with mutually beneficial referrals. The U.S. Bureau of Labor estimates that 48 percent of all jobs come from personal contacts. This reinforces the idea that it is not only *what* you know in business, but also *who* you know.

Consider joining and taking a leadership role in a professional organization such as American Business Women's Association (ABWA), Professional Secretaries International (PSI), Business and Professional Women's Association (BPW), American Association of University Women (AAUW), Federally Employed Women (FEW), National Association of Women Business Owners (NAWBO), National Association of Female Executives (NAFE), or any one of numerous others.

MOVING UP (continued)

It's Not What You Know—It's Who You Know

Of the following ways to improve networking, which could you integrate into your daily activities?

☐ Send congratulation notes or articles of interest

☐ Exchange business cards

☐ Schedule networking breaks or lunches as you would other business meetings

☐ Shake hands and memorize people's names when you meet them for the first time

☐ Share information, resources, referrals and contacts

Networking is a system of unconditional trade-offs. If you ask someone for a favor, offer to return the favor and follow through if they ask for something in return.

EXERCISE: NETWORKING

List two people you could benefit from knowing better:

1. _____

2. _____

List two organizations you should join:

1. _____

2. _____

List two activities that you could use to network:

1. _____

2. _____

Tomorrow you will: _____

_____

_____

Mentors and Role Models

Mentors and role models are two closely linked concepts that can be beneficial when applied to a corporate setting. A *mentor* is someone, such as a teacher, supervisor, coworker or friend, who either knows more than you or has more experience than you, is an inspiration, and is willing to share their wisdom. Many successful people can point to one person who adopted them early in their careers and helped them learn the complexities of business. A mentor can help you chart a path up the corporate ladder or provide a consultation on a specific problem.

Mentors do not feel threatened by younger or newer managers, or by women or men. Rather, they are willing to help others who share their ideals.

Who could you mentor? _____

Who has served as your past mentors? _____

Who could serve as a potential future mentor? _____

What can you do to facilitate the process? _____

A *role model* is someone whose behavior, attitude, image and/or performance sets an example that we want to emulate in our lives. Identify two of your past or current role models.

Why did you select them? _____

What qualities or actions influenced you to select them as role models?

_____

Do you see yourself as a role model? _____

Why or why not? _____

IMAGE

Fair or not, we form a lasting impression within minutes of meeting someone, based on looks, manners, grooming or verbal ability. The way people see you is your image. Image is a major factor in achieving professional success. Some companies even have unwritten dress codes. Women, especially, are judged on these criteria, although we may not like it.

Image also includes proper grammar skills, verbal as well as written.

Image Builders to Consider

Follow the leader.
Follow the established dress code. Also, notice who arrives early and stays late; adjust your schedule so they see that you have adopted their values for punctuality.

Separate your business and personal life.
Casual talk about personal problems or ailments blurs the lines between professional and social relationships.

Convert problems to opportunities.
When you share concerns or problems, share the impact and solution for improving it, as well as the actual situation.

Control your temper at all times.
Impatient or rough language may be overheard and interpreted as inappropriate. Keep your cool, regardless of how angry you are. The old World War II saying, "Loose lips sink ships," applies to most situations.

Pay attention to social obligations within a business context.
If you ask a colleague to lunch, pick up the tab, regardless of your guest's gender. If your colleague buys, send a same-day thank you, even if an expense account has been tapped.

Greet colleagues and customers.
Graciously acknowledge extra efforts and pleasant attitudes. "Please" and "thank you" could possibly be our two most underused words.

Practice impeccable manners, etiquette and protocol, any time, anywhere.
You represent your organization, 24 hours a day, as the best your company has to offer. Manners can enhance opportunities and the lack of them can sabotage your success; you may never even know why.

KEYS TO YOUR SUCCESS

Image—Does your image fit your aspirations? Are you dressing for the job you want? First impressions can be lasting; over 65 percent of our impression is based solely on appearance. Fair or not, we judge abilities on appearance. What messages are your clothes, manners, body language and voice conveying? Have you compared your perception with your manager's perception of you? An investment in your image is an investment in your career.

Attitude—Attitude is a choice. The one you send is usually the one you get back. Give yourself an attitude check. Do you:

- ☐ Lose your temper easily, get discouraged easily by small setbacks, or seem moody?

- ☐ If your face froze, would you like what you saw in the mirror?

- ☐ Do you complain or join in with the complainers, or do you actively seek ways to improve situations?

Performance—Managers should set the standard for performance. Know and do what is expected of you. Set goals and objectives and follow them. Lead by example. Follow only those who set a high standard for performance. Give more than 100 percent.

People Skills—Never underestimate the value of anyone because of their position or status. Earn the trust of the people you work with and for; give trust, respect and accountability, demonstrate your confidence in the team's ability, allow for mistakes or setbacks, and recognize and reward those who contribute ideas or participate in change. Involve those who will be affected by or contribute to a decision. Above all, keep your sense of humor.

Despite obstacles and negative attitudes toward women in management, women *are* moving up. Mentoring, networking, and bypassing are three primary techniques utilized to build the contacts, support, and influence needed. While possessing the image, attitude, performance and people skills are essential, success will also necessitate initiative and ease with business protocol and difficult situations. The suggestions in this section will provide you with valuable information to help you on your journey to the top.

PART

II

Essential Management Skills

- Time Management
- Communicating for Results
- Negotiation
- Making Decisions and Solving Problems

TIME MANAGEMENT

> *"I have yet to hear a man ask for advice on how to combine marriage and a career."*
>
> Gloria Steinem (1934–   )
> American feminist and journalist

If you are feeling overwhelmed, frustrated and powerless to accomplish what needs to be done this week, you are not alone. If you are tired of carrying the load, why not try a different approach to managing your time for increased results and satisfaction?

Women in business have a sword of Damocles hanging over their heads. Not only are they expected to perform well at their workplace, they are also expected to continue doing the stereotypically *female* chores at home, such as cooking, cleaning, washing and childcare. Unless they can afford a maid or a nanny, or have an unusual mate, women still carry the burden of household responsibilities.

Working women typically spend at least 15 more hours each week performing household chores than their male counterparts. If you are married and seem to do all the housework, consider having a family conference about sharing household chores.

The Importance of Time Management

To improve time management, begin by asking the following questions:

► Where does my time go? Do I use my time effectively?

► What values and quality of life issues—personal and professional—are important? How can I balance, prioritize and fulfill them?

► What kind of relationship do I want to have with my mate? How does it compare with the kind of relationship that my mate wants?

► How can all household members more fully contribute to the household responsibilities?

TIME WASTERS AT HOME

Time management is as important at home as it is in the office.

At-Home Quick Check

Place a ''✓'' beside each of the following suggestions that you could implement immediately. Place a ''+'' beside each that you already employ:

☐ Rise 15 or 20 minutes before other household members, to catch a few private minutes to outline the days priorities, organize or just read the news.

☐ Take another 15 or 20 minutes before retiring in the evening to plan or organize the next day's activities, select clothing, gain a headstart on meal preparation, and to reflect positively on the day's gifts.

☐ When you arrive home, take 15 or 20 minutes to share highlights of your day with household members, or to simply make the transition. Every hour you invest in planning can potentially save three to four hours in actually performing the tasks; the gains in nurturing relationships can prove immeasurable.

☐ When matching tasks to household members, open all tasks to members by preference, rather than by those historically considered *male* or *female jobs,* such as mowing the lawn or loading the dishwasher. If we expect this at work, it follows that we should provide similar opportunities at home:

— Prepare and share a list of all weekly responsibilities with all household members.

— Allow household members to choose tasks according to personal preference and best day.

— Allow household members to propose their own accountability, rewards or sanctions.

Allowing others to set their own standards often results in higher standards than those that would have been set for them, whether at home or at work.

TIME WASTERS AT WORK

If your priorities are not being achieved, identify time wasters such as:

Interruptions

Unscheduled Meetings

Drop-In Visitors

Time wasters fall basically into two categories—internal and external.

Time Waster Checklist

Internal time wasters are actions that you can control, such as personal traits or work habits.	**External time wasters** are events or items that you cannot control.
Place a ''✓'' by each time waster that sabotages your efforts.	
☐ Procrastination	☐ Telephone calls
☐ Inadequate delegation	☐ Meetings
☐ Failure to plan	☐ Visitors
☐ Poor scheduling	☐ Paperwork
☐ Lack of self-discipline	☐ Inadequately trained staff
☐ Attempting to do too much	☐ Lack of policies and procedures
☐ Lack of relevant skills	

MEETINGS

Do you feel you spend all your time in meetings and can only get your work done at home, on nights and on weekends? Today, most managerial work is accomplished through the ten million plus business meetings held every business day. Our 1990s style is participative management, involving all levels in decision-making and problem-solving by committees, teams or quality circles.

It is especially important for women to lead and participate in meetings, to showcase their leadership skills and managerial potential. As more mid-level positions are eliminated in favor of teams, it is crucial that women develop meeting skills to gain additional experience, responsibilities, visibility and exposure. Consider volunteering for key project teams; teams can afford you a unique opportunity to develop a wide range of contacts and resources.

Most managers spend 15 percent or more of their time in meetings and about one-half of that time is wasted. Incorporate the following tips, to make meetings more productive and less wasteful.

Before the Meeting

Outline the meeting's purpose and objectives. Before preparing the agenda, list topics that need to be discussed, decisions that need to be reached and questions that need to be answered. Invite members who have the knowledge, ability and influence to achieve the objectives and accomplish the necessary tasks.

Agenda

Use a one-page agenda or meeting outline (see sample on page 44). Your agenda should support the meeting's objectives and include names of those who will attend the meeting, the start and end time, the place of the meeting, and prioritized items according to importance and amount of allotted time for discussion. Whenever possible, distribute the agenda two days to a week before the meeting.

As a team member, know in advance which parts of the agenda you are responsible for, and any other preparation that is required of you.

AGENDA ITEMS

*Team Leader:*_____   *Date Submitted:*_____

_____   _____
Name of Group to Meet   *Date of Meeting*

1. Topic or issue for discussion in specific terms

2. The problem is: (State the problem in specific terms and provide an example with facts if helpful to clarify.)

3. Causes of the problem are:

4. Possible solutions are:

5. The best solution is:

6. Action to be taken:

After the meeting, as the teamleader or meeting recorder, summarize the discussion in one page. Communicate the topics discussed, persons and date of action assigned, and decisions reached. The ''Meeting Follow-Up Guide'' on page 45 can be useful as you prepare your discussion notes. Distribute your discussion notes within two days of the meeting.

Meeting Notes

DATE _____

TIME _____

PLACE _____

PAGE _____ OF _____

OF PEOPLE _____

☐ Route to _____
☐ Please note and file
☐ For your information
☐ Please note & forward to _____
☐ Please take charge of this
☐ Your comments, please
☐ RUSH—IMMEDIATE ACTION
   REQUIRED

PURPOSE/TOPIC _____

PEOPLE INVOLVED		
NAME	**TITLE**	**DEPARTMENT**
1.		
2.		
3.		
4.		

ISSUES DISCUSSED _____

_____

_____

_____

_____

_____

ACTION NEEDED _____

_____

_____

_____

_____

ASSIGNMENT(S) MADE		
NAME	**DUE DATE**	**DATE COMPLETED**

COMMENTS _____

_____

_____

Meeting Follow-Up Guide

MINUTES

Name of Group: _____ Meeting Title: _____

Purpose of Meeting: _____

Facilitator: _____ EXT # _____

Who Attended:

_____   _____
_____   _____
_____   _____

AGENDA (Attached)

Summary of the Issues:

```
┌─────────────────────────────────────────────────────┐
│                                                     │
│                                                     │
│                                                     │
│                                                     │
│                                                     │
└─────────────────────────────────────────────────────┘
```

What Was Decided:

```
┌─────────────────────────────────────────────────────┐
│                                                     │
│                                                     │
│                                                     │
│                                                     │
│                                                     │
└─────────────────────────────────────────────────────┘
```

Next Meeting: _____ Date: _____ Place: _____

ACTION PLAN:

WHAT WILL BE DONE	WHO WILL DO IT	BY WHEN

Suggestions:
- *Summarize just what was in the meeting. Keep your summary brief so people will read it—outline form is good.*
- *If there was disagreement, include options from both sides.*
- *Do not edit or interpret.*
- *Use people's comments and ideas as they were originally expressed.*
- *Try to make the summary interesting to read*
- *Get it out as soon as possible after the meeting.*

THE PAPER TRAIL

If you find you spend increasing amounts of time on the process, such as paperwork, and less time with customers or employees, now is the time to empower yourself to shorten the paper trail.

Paperwork Quick Check

Which of the following techniques would be helpful to incorporate into your habits? Place a "✓" besides those you will incorporate within the next seven days; place a "+" beside each technique that you currently employ:

☐ Edit, combine, simplify and eliminate processes and paper by questioning the purpose, value and cost of each piece of paper that crosses your desk. Ask others to do the same.

☐ Commit to only one project or paper on your desk at a time. Work from a master list. File the rest to allow yourself the necessary focus and concentration.

☐ Impose a one-page policy for letters and memos.

☐ Either do, delegate or dump any piece of paper you pick up, by attempting to take immediate action. By taking immediate action, you eliminate wasted time looking at the same tasks over and over.

☐ Color-code and consolidate action items—for example, a red basket for signature or urgent items, a green basket for reading, a yellow basket for important but not urgent items.

Files

To maintain an effective filing system, you must keep records up to date and easily retrievable.

Having access to information does not mean having it piled in your face; it means knowing how to find it. Attempt to reduce current files by 20 percent. Question how long items are stored. Move them outside your office, when possible.

Record the date last used in each file. Once a year, remove the files that no one has consulted in the last twelve months, if they are no longer required by company filing policies.

Following are a few tips to help you maintain an effective file-storage system.

- Try to eliminate 20 percent of the material filed, rather than ask for a new filing cabinet.

- Make a new file when you have three pieces of correspondence pertaining to one project.

- Use tickler files with pockets for the twelve months, or for the days in a month. This provides a place for notes to call prospects or meet deadlines.

- Clean off your desk. Do not use your desk as a file cabinet.

Fewer files mean less paperwork to handle when you need to research a fact or review a letter. Less paperwork creates an environment that encourages effective time management and eliminates the overwhelming feelings associated with mounds of filing. A neat desk and organized work area create an image of efficiency.*

_____

For an excellent book on this subject, order *Organizing Your Workspace* by Odette Pollar, Crisp Publications, using the information in the back of this book.

COMMUNICATION

Effective communication skills can be instrumental in saving time. By being able to communicate what you want to the first time, you will eliminate the need to explain or give information a second, third or even fourth time. Give thorough, concise instructions. Invite questions. Do not assume the person you are communicating with will automatically understand or ask questions; he or she may fear appearing unknowledgeable or insensitive to time constraints.

Schedule a status meeting once daily, and once a week with your manager or team leader, assistant or others to update the status of priorities and objectives. Discuss what has been accomplished, what is currently being completed and what work remains.

Learn to set specific times for telephone communication and schedule quiet time to work without phone interruptions. Block out a portion of each day to return calls. To reduce your telephone time, ask or train your assistant to gather as much information as possible about callers. Here are a few other time saving tips for telephone communication:

► Limit calls to three minutes or less as a mental discipline. Pretend you are paying the phone bill.

► Ask friends and family to call only at certain, less hectic times of the day and to refrain from calling unless it is an emergency. Personal calls not only erode productivity, but can also distract fellow employees.

► Schedule critical conversations as you would any other business appointment. Allow no interruptions. Treat telephone calls with the same attention you would give a personal visit to your office.

► To save unnecessary call backs, when placing a call, pull the client file and make notes of questions you must ask and decisions that must be reached.

DELEGATION

Delegation can be one of the most challenging functions of management for women, as they make the transition from employee/associate to manager/teamleader. Many women have long practiced the ''it's easier/faster/better to do it myself'' maxim. The Superwoman Myth, which infers that, without assistance, women can unconditionally fulfill all roles as employee, mate, child, parent and civic worker, is not a myth at all.

Delegating tasks is not relinquishing responsibilities. It is ensuring that the tasks will be accomplished in the most efficient and effective manner. As a manager or teamleader, you are accountable for the results, not by how much was personally completed. Learn to let go of the methods or approach by which someone accomplishes tasks that you especially like or perform well; give them the authority, and trust them. It is not an easy process, but it is an essential one for any aspiring woman manager.

Delegation, then, is the act of assigning work to an individual or team, empowering them with the authority or right to act or to make decisions, as well as giving them the responsibility for the decisions and actions.

To determine if your ability to delegate could improve, ask yourself the following questions. Place a ''✓'' by all that apply to you.

☐ Do you frequently complete a job because you can do it better or faster than someone else?

☐ Do your associates often perform much of their work over, or a second time?

☐ Do you find yourself bogged down with details, unable to allocate sufficient time to planning and developing?

☐ Do you continue to complete tasks because you enjoy them, even though someone else has the ability or responsibility?

DELEGATION (continued)

If you answered ''yes'' to one or more of the previous questions, consider implementing the following suggestions. To identify some of your responsibilities that can be handled by others, answer the following questions:

- What tasks can or should be delegated?

- If you provided additional training or instructions, could you delegate additional tasks?

- What tasks could your manager delegate to you that he or she does not perform well, does not like to do, could be completed by you with appropriate training, or could be beneficial to your growth and development?

The following chart will help you compile your answers. In the next seven days, why not share your list with your manager, associates, assistant, or team.

Delegation Record

Key Results Area	Results Expected	Who Can Do It For Me Now	Who Can Be Trained	Assigned To	Follow-up Required

To track results of delegated assignments of individuals or teams, consider using a delegation tracking list. (See sample form below.) On it you can note estimated time for completion, target date, results and resources needed. This tool can be used to delegate to an individual group, such as a team or department. It can also be used by one individual who reports to more than one boss, as well as for organizing tasks that require assistance from others.

Delegation Tracking System

Task	Person	Date/Time Assigned	Date/Time Due	Date/Time Received	Resources Needed	Results Comments

Focus on priorities and set realistic expectations to create a sense of confidence and satisfaction. By taking responsibility for improving our own work habits, we may see our employer, or our job and our future, from an improved perspective. In simplest terms, not delegating is not managing. Responsibility to improve follows our awareness of the need to do so.

COMMUNICATING FOR RESULTS

> *"Success is turning knowledge into positive action."*
>
> Dorothy Leeds (1939–   )
> Author of *Smart Questions: New Strategies for Successful Management*, Berkeley Publishing, 1988.

We spend two-thirds of our day communicating. We correct misunderstandings, act on misinformation, deal with rumors and gossip, or do a job over a second or third time. This chapter addresses communication and ways to improve both written and verbal communication skills.

The woman manager should be aware that traditional female communication patterns that taught women to "act and speak like a lady" may undermine their credibility and effectiveness. Such patterns include:

✔ **Using tag questions and disclaimers**

Overusing words such as "hope" and "try." For example: "I hope to complete my degree in 1994." Or, "I'll try to complete the report." Or, "I think we should establish a project team to reduce our delivery time, don't you think?"

✔ **Apologizing unnecessarily**

For example, "I'm sorry the marketing manager was unable to submit the report on time." Apologize only when you sincerely regret a mistake or event over which you had control but failed to act properly. Distinguish between those events that you *do* and *do not* have control over; decide whether *admit* or *regret* is a better word choice than *sorry*.

✔ **Use qualifiers**

Use words or phrases like "kinda," "sorta," "hope," "guess," "I'm not sure . . . but"—sparingly, to avoid sounding uncertain or uncommitted. It is imperative that women speak confidently, deliberately and distinctively. They should use assertive language, comfortable eye contact, listen effectively and provide direct feedback. These behaviors help to avoid the misconception that they are dependent or insecure. In *Success and Sounding Competitive,* by Sarah Hordesty and Nehana Jacobs, one recent psychological study revealed that women make special efforts to convince their bosses that they are competent. On the other hand, male managers try to reassure their bosses that they are not competing for the same job and do not want to appear overly confident.

✔ **Allowing interruptions**

Studies show that men more freely interrupt women who are speaking, talk more than women, and dominate meetings. Women can tactfully handle such situations. A response such as ''Excuse me, John, but I'd like to finish my remark,'' can aid the woman manager. Or, a woman manager might prepare comments or one-liners before meetings. If women want power, they need to communicate with power.

Also you should clearly communicate the purposes, standards, policies, instructions, objectives, deadlines, priorities, expected feedback or follow-up required.

Common Communication Blocks

#1 Poor timing

#2 Incomplete information

#3 Distractions

#4 Emotional interference

#5 Premature judgment

#6 Incorrect channel

#7 Misjudging your audience

#8 Assuming once is enough

COMMON COMMUNICATIONS BLOCKS

#1 POOR TIMING

A message's timing may be as important as its content. For example, sensitivity to best and worst times, before asking for additional resources or selling an idea, enhances the possibility of acceptance.

#2 INCOMPLETE INFORMATION

Provide accurate, concise and complete information. Including the reasons or purpose is essential for effective communication. Ask questions, summarize and paraphrase information to ensure accuracy and avoid incorrect assumptions.

#3 DISTRACTIONS

Ringing telephones, equipment such as computers and copiers, background music and conversations are distracting. Move to a more private place to avoid miscommunicating.

#4 EMOTIONAL INTERFERENCE

With the increasing need to accomplish more in less time, people feel pressured and anxious about responsibilities and deadlines. Focus, prioritize and be aware of the effect of emotions on your ability to communicate.

#5 PREMATURE JUDGMENT

Because an average listener can process 400 words per minute and speak at 200 words per minute, your listener may reach a conclusion before you have made all your important points. Clarify and organize your ideas before you communicate. As a listener, give your full concentration to the speaker, without interrupting the speaker, and clarify any unclear points.

#6 INCORRECT CHANNEL

Choose a written channel, such as a memo or letter, when you need documentation, proof, or must record more detailed information. If you anticipate getting a reaction, be prepared to discuss the information.

#7 MISJUDGING YOUR AUDIENCE

Like a good reporter, find out who needs or wants to know this information. What is the situation? What is the background? Avoid sending information unless it meets such criteria; this shows respect for others' time, as well as for your own.

#8 ASSUMING ONCE IS ENOUGH

When you write a memo, or mention a situation in a meeting, behavior does not automatically change. Support your communications by repeating the message in a variety of ways. Positively reinforce even modest changes or improvements.

Know your objective and your audience, organize your thoughts, compensate for distractions, give complete information, and be sensitive to timing and emotions. These will all help overcome communication blocks.

EXERCISE

Place a "✓" beside each of the following communication tips on which you could improve in the next seven days:

- ☐ Actively listen
- ☐ Ask questions
- ☐ Think before speaking
- ☐ Check for understanding
- ☐ Follow up your communication, when appropriate

PRESENTATIONS

Making presentations can enhance your visibility and opportunities in any job. While a few people profess to be born public speakers, most admit that they had to overcome fears about speaking in front of a group. They must practice relentlessly before gaining the necessary confidence.

Be so *well prepared* for any presentation that you can give the speech spontaneously. **Rehearse** in front of a mirror, with a tape recorder or video camera running. Practice your speech or presentation aloud, since reading your material will take less time than vocalizing it. **Time** your speech to ensure it fits the allotted program time. Note the words that are difficult to enunciate. If you use a podium, avoid clutching it. White knuckles kill a presentation.

Use open-hand gestures to emphasize your main points. Do not overdo your gestures, though; they may detract from your presentation.

Analyze your audience in terms of age, sex, income, education, special concerns, and interests. This will help you determine the appropriate tone, humor and approach.

Practice at every opportunity. Practice may not make perfect, but it will make presentations easier.

COMMUNICATING WITH YOUR MANAGER OR TEAM LEADER

Your manager or team leader wants to be informed of your progress on tasks and projects and of your problems.

When sharing your progress, offer not only what has been accomplished, but what you are currently working on, any conflicting priorities and deadlines, and what remains to be done.

Record all assignments on the Delegation Tracking System on page 63. This provides an overview for your manager to help you re-prioritize. It also helps you to plan and consolidate tasks more easily.

Written Communication

Written communication should be:

Conversational—Write in a friendly manner, avoiding complicated phrases.

Correct—Check facts, grammar, spelling and punctuation.

Concise—Use short, easy-to-read paragraphs and one-page memos, letters and summaries.

Complete—Provide all necessary facts such as who, what, when, where, why and how, and any related dates or numerical data.

Are you frequently frustrated by rereading correspondence several times to discern the action required of you, the reader? When writing memos and letters, state the purpose or objective in the first sentence. Provide the details in the body. Then, summarize by stating the action required in the last sentence. Eliminating the mystery in correspondence saves valuable time and prevents errors.

Are you dismayed with people who make promises that they forget to keep? Make it a habit to record your communications, on a *promise pad* or in a *journal*. Note what action was promised, when and by whom.

With ever-increasing workloads, effective communication has become more than a needed skill. It is our opportunity to improve relations.

ASSERTIVENESS TRAINING

In her book, *YOU JUST DON'T UNDERSTAND: Women and Men in Conversation*, Deborah Tannen, Ph.D., says that many women are reluctant to boast about their achievements to others. They fear people will not like them if they do. Childhood conditioning taught that it is not ladylike to boast.

If you do not share achievements with others, you are likely to be underestimated and passed over for promotions. All new managers need to be assertive; women managers especially need to set the correct tones for their management styles.

When was the last time you stood in line and someone cut in front of you? How did you react? Did you huff and puff, stare and glare, as if to say, "How dare you?" How long have you been meaning to express a few concerns to your boss, share new ideas or ask for more responsibilities—maybe even a raise?

We all encounter many stressful situations. How we handle them affects not only our professional effectiveness, but also our personal sense of self-esteem.

Assertiveness training is a solution that will enhance your ability to communicate more effectively. Assertiveness is based on the idea that by changing your actions, you can change your attitude and feelings.

The following information summarizes the differences between assertive, non-assertive and aggressive behavior.

> **Assertiveness** is standing up for your rights in an open, honest and direct way, which does not violate another person's rights. You have a responsibility to ask for what you want, make your feelings and opinions known, and act in a manner worthy of respect.

> **Nonassertiveness** is allowing your rights to be violated, by failing to express your feelings or submitting to another person's needs or wants at your own expense.

> **Aggressive** behavior is determining a certain outcome, without considering anyone else's opinion or permission. Aggressive behavior is expressing feelings or stating wants in a manner that is dishonest, demeaning, patronizing, overwhelming, domineering or dominating.

The chart below compares Assertive, Nonassertive and Aggressive communication characteristics.

Behavior Characteristics

Assertive	Nonassertive	Aggressive
Has clear boundaries and does not allow others to restrict or violate them.	Allows boundaries to be restricted or violated.	Invades others' boundaries.
Lets others know clearly thoughts or desires.	Fails to express honest feelings, beliefs or thoughts at appropriate times.	Expresses feelings or beliefs in a way which is often dishonest, inappropriate, overbearing or pushy.
Expresses affection and appreciation.	Seeks permission to do something or give opinion.	Blames, accuses and puts others down.
Strong eye contact, erect posture, firmly planted feet, natural gestures.	Slumped posture, shifting weight, evasive eye contact, nervous mannerisms.	Cold stares, finger pointing, hands on hips, clenched fists, tense posture.

You cannot become more assertive simply by reading this section. The next step is a personal choice—to practice, learn and apply the assertive communication skills. In addition to enriching your professional and personal relationships, you will enjoy the process more, and accomplish more in less time, with less stress. You might even have more friends.

Assertiveness Quick Check

From the list below, place a "✓" beside those areas in which it will be advantageous to become more assertive. Under each item, list at least one specific activity that you will complete to become more assertive. Place a "+" beside the areas in which you excel in demonstrating your assertive skills.

☐ Assume responsibility for your actions and mistakes.

_____

☐ Identify what bothers you; instead, share how you feel, what you want or expect.

_____

☐ Set limits on what is expected from you.

_____

☐ Identify communication responses in others. If you do not agree with their response, mentally *replay it* to create a more appropriate response.

_____

☐ Encourage others to be assertive. Allow them to express their feelings and opinions.

_____

☐ Learn to say "no."

_____

☐ Ask for what you want. Do not expect anyone to read your mind.

_____

EXERCISE: PRACTICE AND APPLY ASSERTIVENESS

How would you respond in each of the following three situations?
Record your dialogue for each option.

1. One of your team members has missed the last three project
meetings. As the teamleader, how will you respond to this team
member; what will you say?

Aggressive: _____

Nonassertive: _____

Assertive: _____

2. Your manager discovers an error, and shouts in front of your
associates, ''How could you be that stupid!'' How will you respond?

Aggressive: _____

Nonassertive: _____

Assertive: _____

3. While you are having lunch with a team member, the team member
lights a cigarette. You find cigarette smoke offensive. What will you
say?

Aggressive: _____

Nonassertive: _____

Assertive: _____

ASSERTIVENESS TRAINING (continued)

Choose Assertiveness to Win

Simply by sharing your desires, you have a 50–50 chance of getting what you want. Assertiveness is a philosophy that is based on the following beliefs:

- Express appreciation, starting with "please" and "thank you."

- Know your rights, such as:

    ✔ You have the right to say "no."

    ✔ You have the right to ask for what you want.

    ✔ You have the right to disagree.

    ✔ You have the right to your feelings. Others may disagree with your opinions, but they cannot disagree with your feelings.

    ✔ You have the right to be treated with respect.

    ✔ You have the right to have your ideas heard.

    ✔ You have the right to be listened to.

Every relationship involves each person having 50 percent of the responsibility for the success or failure of the relationship. Although we cannot be responsible for the thoughts, feelings, opinions, habits or behaviors of others, we do have responsibility for our own.

Assertiveness is a choice. While nonassertiveness or even aggressiveness may be a more appropriate response in some situations, overall assertiveness is the preferred communication style. It fosters and builds strong relationships, confidence and self-esteem.

NEGOTIATION

> *"Remember, no one can make you feel inferior without your consent."*
>
> Eleanor Roosevelt (1884–1962)
> Humanitarian and writer, wife of President Franklin Delano Roosevelt

While men tend to focus on winning, valuing independence and competition, our tendency as women is to focus on collaboration for long-term interaction. This will serve us well in leading our chosen organizations.

In *Megatrends for Women*, Morrow, 1990, Lester Korn of Korn/Ferry states, "Women in some industries are, well, managerial bargains. Some clients realize they save 25 to 30 percent by hiring women. We see it in executive searches all the time."

You probably need to develop negotiating skills to succeed as a woman manager. If you like to . . .

Avoid conflicts and confrontations

Be popular and well-liked

Accept whatever is offered

Avoid haggling over details such as money or titles

Then you will settle for less than the best.

On the other hand, you are on your way to being a seasoned negotiator if you like . . .

To settle differences

To think under pressure

To express yourself and your opinions

To challenge your communication skills to persuade others

NEGOTIATION (continued)

What Do You Want?

As with every business transaction, negotiation starts with knowing what you want to gain.

Using skills gained in the discussion of goal setting in Part I, write down the best possible outcome of the discussion. Be as specific as possible in verbalizing your needs and desires. This could be the $100-a-week raise, the title of Office Manager, authorization to proceed with your plan, or anything else you want to have after the negotiation concludes. Clarify your goal, so that it stays foremost in your mind throughout the preparation and final negotiation.

Next write down your "fall-back" position. A fall-back position is the minimum area, in a range of concessions, in which you are willing to compromise in the negotiation process.

Part of analyzing negotiations in advance is to evaluate the negotiation potential of each person and each situation. Negotiation potential is the ability of a person or situation to effect a change. A person has negotiation potential if she has the opportunity to ask for a raise or the authority to grant one. If you are in a position to deal or to offer something in exchange for receiving something else, you have negotiation potential.

NEGOTIATING A WIN-WIN SOLUTION

WIN-WIN situations can evolve in a variety of ways:

► **A compromise**—Both sides leave the meeting after achieving at least one goal. Both sides have given in to at least one of the opposition's demands, but neither side has surrendered to every demand that was made originally. A compromise is actually a third plan, created somewhere between each side's position.

► **Save face**—Both sides feel positive about the decision, since no one has to admit a previous bad decision or take blame for a certain course of action. Instead, both parties leave with the feeling of a moral victory, because of a new plan or outcome. Issuing ultimatums negates any chance of saving face; instead of ordering the opposing side to ''do this or else,'' saving face means offering the other side a range of choices, all of which provide favorable outcomes for yourself.

► **Collaboration**—Instead of embracing one solution completely, the outcome includes portions of each person's plan, to make the outcome a joint effort. Both sides share in the new hybrid plan as a partnership, instead of one person receiving the credit. Pride and ego can derail attempts at collaborations. Collaborations can only work if both sides are willing to follow a certain course of action, without regard to who receives the credit.

► **A trade-out**—Each party agrees to give up something, to gain something else. For example, a manager might forego capital improvements to her office to gain a cost-of-living raise for the department. A trade-out is more likely to involve tangible assets such as money, titles, equipment, office space or employment benefits, rather than ideas. A trade-out can be a win-win situation, because both parties have something to use in bargaining. Both have the opportunity to complete negotiations in a better position than they started. Identify what is truly important to your cause, and/or what you are willing to give up to receive something else.

► **Take advantage of the situation**—If you sense that your opponent is underestimating you, because you are a woman or because you represent a minority, do not take it personally. Use this as an opportunity to obtain your desired result, often without the other person realizing how much he/she has given up.

NEGOTIATING A WIN-WIN SOLUTION (continued)

▶ **Realize that being told "no" is not the end of the world.** Remind yourself that the disapproval for the raise or promotion you have requested is not intended for you personally. Working through fear of rejection helps take the anxiety out of negotiations.

▶ **Do not be defensive or offensive.** Know that you are not alone in your uncertainty in facing negotiation. Most supervisors would also like to grant every request to avoid confrontation.

▶ **Select your turf when you negotiate.** Select your territory, such as your own desk or office, to enhance your security during negotiations. If you want to be able to plant an idea and walk away, consider going to the other person's office; then you can leave at will. For informal negotiations, look for neutral places such as a coffee shop or lounge area, that are nonthreatening to either person.

▶ **When appropriate, try to get a decision on the spot.** Giving the other person too much time may allow them to think of new reasons why you should not receive your request. If you want something specific, attempt to get an answer within a specific time. If the listener promises to consider the request later, keep pressing for a specific time such as a month or six weeks in which to have an answer. If you let the issue become indefinitely prolonged, you risk losing the negotiation to added red tape or other layers of a corporate bureaucracy. In addition, your arguments may become diluted or irrelevant after some time has passed. Confirm the agreed upon time in a memo for written confirmation.

▶ **Avoid ultimatums.** If you ask for only one thing "or else," you may be disappointed when your opponent selects the "or else." By giving an ultimatum, you create a situation where the opponent can only pick one alternative. Many supervisors resent being backed into a corner with statements of "If I can't have a raise, I quit" or "If you are going to promote her over me, you'll be making a mistake." Besides the resentment, you may have offered a plan that is impossible. Then, the supervisor has no choice but to accept your resignation on the spot.

Successful negotiations are the result of being prepared and knowing what objectives you want to achieve. Define your goals, clarify the issues involved, and be prepared to compromise. Any negotiation, properly conducted, can be an opportunity for both parties to win.

MAKING DECISIONS AND SOLVING PROBLEMS

> *"Security is mostly a superstition. It does not exist in nature . . ."*
>
> Helen Keller (1880–1968)
> American essayist and lecturer

Making 60 to 80 decisions in a typical day and spending two-thirds of your day preventing or correcting potential situations or dealing with difficult people can be overwhelming.

As a manager, one of your prime responsibilities is to prevent and resolve problems that could become roadblocks for your staff. If you have trouble making decisions that keep your department or team running smoothly, your attitude or approach can undermine your best intentions.

As a woman manager, expect some additional challenges dealing with preconceived attitudes or myths about women as decision makers. Myths still prevail about women's decision-making ability—such as "too emotional to make decisions," "cannot make decisions due to lack of business experience." These are usually based on trends from decades to centuries ago, when women stayed at home like Cinderella, waiting for their Prince Charming to arrive, to announce his next decision or preference. Decision-making and problem solving are skills we learn and improve, and our ability to make sound decisions is not based on sex—it is based on ability, intuition and experience.

In today's business environment, characterized by the bombardment of rapid changes, decision-making and problem solving are crucial skills for the woman manager. Instead of worrying about what other people think, or getting too much advice from those who may or may not be involved, realize that there is seldom only one acceptable choice in solving a situation. Regardless of our uncertainty about the desired outcome or lack of support from others, we cannot depend on others to make decisions for us. It is our responsibility to make decisions, follow through, and expect and prepare for both positive and negative consequences.

MAKING DECISIONS AND SOLVING PROBLEMS (continued)

One of the most challenging duties of being a manager is counseling an associate about a problem. Here are a few tips for these difficult discussions.

1. Be kind and let the employee know you are concerned for his/her well-being. Identify the employee's problem in a nonthreatening way. Do not try to be a psychiatrist or social worker.

2. Select a private place to let the employee know how the problem is affecting him/her or the team's performance.

3. Ask your associate to come up with a solution. Ask questions such as:

   • How would you describe the situation?

   • What do you think caused the situation?

   • What do you see as the problem?

   • What solutions do you recommend?

   • What are you willing to do to correct, prevent or improve the situation?

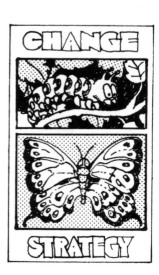

DECISION-MAKING TECHNIQUES

Use the following techniques to generate alternatives or solutions:

Random Brainstorming

Any team member shares an idea, which the recorder records on flip-chart for all team members to see.

Round-Robin Brainstorming

Team members present their ideas in sequence, moving from one person to the next. Each team member gives only one idea at a turn; if a team member does not have an idea, he/she may pass. The process continues until all ideas are exhausted.

Silent Generation

Team members write their ideas on a brainstorming form, instead of talking to each other. Each team member writes three ideas across the top row of a paper, then places his or her paper in the center of a table. Members select other forms, adding three different ideas to each until ideas are exhausted. If members sit at multiple tables, a facilitator can swap forms between tables.

The Delphi Technique

Team members independently complete a series of questionnaires concerning problems or issues. The team leader collects and tabulates other people's written opinions, without discussion or debate. Written answers and feedback determine the best solution.

Factual feedback of results is provided to the members. If needed, team members complete another round of questionnaires and receive feedback until significant agreement is reached among panel members. A final report is written that presents the results of the process.

DECISION-MAKING TECHNIQUES
(continued)

Team Advantages

Using a team approach to problem solving provides a wide range of creativity and information, since each team member brings different skills and perspective. It builds morale, productivity, quality, team spirit and commitment, because team members share in the decision-making process, in an area that affects them as individuals.

Team Disadvantages

Using a team approach also has disadvantages. One disadvantage is the time consideration; a team member may be under time constraints and have to take time from another important project to make time for the team meeting. There is also the chance that one team member will dominate the process and/or have a hidden agenda to further his or her own position.

PROBLEM SOLVING

To gain visibility and enhance your contribution to your organization, make it a practice to recommend solutions to problems or make suggestions for improving present conditions or procedures both informally to managers or teamleaders, and formally utilizing the company's suggestion system. If your company does not have a suggestion system, why not suggest one.

Suggestion Form

Name _____ Date _____

Address _____ Phone # _____

  I. Suggestion: _____

_____

_____

     Present condition or procedure: _____

_____

     Proposed condition or procedure: _____

_____

_____

     Specific benefits/Cost savings: _____

_____

     How it can be implemented/solution: _____

_____

  II. Manager's response: _____

_____

_____

 III. Reviewed by: _____

     Received on: _____

     Forwarded to: _____ Date _____

TECHNIQUES FOR EFFECTIVE PROBLEM SOLVING

Whether a problem is simple or complex, arriving at the solution requires basic steps. The solution to any problem will revolve around the six major points of the Problem-Solving Approach, outlined below.

Problem-Solving Approach

STEP 1. In a comprehensive, concise manner, describe the facts, effects and consequences of the situation.

STEP 2. Identify the cause/problem and recognize the symptoms.

STEP 3. List the facts—who, what, when, where, why and how.

STEP 4. Propose alternative solutions to the problem.

STEP 5. Make a recommendation.

STEP 6. Prepare an action plan and note what action will be taken, by whom, and what can be done to prevent the problem from reoccurring.

CASE STUDY

Read the following situation and use the problem-solving approach to answer the following questions. If you choose to work as a team in a group of two or more, try one or more of the brainstorming techniques to solve the problem.

> Janice has worked for Better Boxes, Inc.. for four years as a customer-service representative, but was recently promoted to customer-service manager and transferred to your area as a result of a corporate reorganization. Although she has never managed before, she will supervise three new representatives, one of whom is her best friend, Alice. Since Janice's promotion, Alice has come in late, left work early without notice, and is taking longer than the hour allowed for lunch. Janice comes to you as her manager for advice.

1. Restate the facts. _____
   _____

2. What are the problem's causes and symptoms? _____
   _____

3. In two or three sentences, summarize and describe the situation according to your perception. _____
   _____

4. What are two or three possible solutions? _____
   _____

5. What is your overall recommendation? _____
   _____

Regardless of the techniques or approaches used to make decisions or solve problems, recommendations or solutions should favorably answer three questions:

    1. Is it good for the company?

    2. Is it good for the customer?

    3. Is it good for the employee?

P A R T

III

Get on Top and Stay There

- Understanding Power and Politics
- Managing Stress

UNDERSTANDING POWER AND POLITICS

> *"Being powerful is like being a lady. If you have to tell people you are, you aren't."*
>
> Margaret Thatcher, (1925–   )
> Former prime minister of Great Britain

Cultural conditioning may have reinforced women to believe that power is "unladylike." Yet, it is essential that aspiring women managers understand the important role of power in effective performance.

For example, boys learn to put winning ahead of relationships, and to "play by the rules" of the situation. They suppress their individuality for the greater good of the team; they play competitive games that teach them to protect their feelings of self-worth, at the expense of relationships. Girls learn to value cooperation and relationships. Historically, they have not been encouraged to play sports that teach the "rules of the game," as boys do. Many girls grew up playing "mommy" to dolls and learning household duties. Most young females were encouraged to foster long-term relationships, as well as to defer to others' needs.

Both sexes lost something in the transition from childhood to adulthood. Now, men are learning to get in touch with the feminine side of their personalities; women are learning how to function on higher levels in male-dominated businesses.

Being courteous and assertive, gaining the support of decision makers, building support through networking, discouraging overprotective male managers, and sharing information with others, all enhance the woman manager's personal power.

Powerful People

- Get the job done with no excuses

- Keep their commitments and promises

- Gain cooperation or resources by using their authority

- Are enthusiastic and energetic

- Make things happen, persuade, change and influence

UNDERSTANDING POWER AND POLITICS (continued)

Types of Power

✔ **Position power**—The ability to exercise the assigned legitimate authority inherent in the job description, title and specifications.

✔ **Reward power**—The ability to confer rewards or positive reinforcement.

✔ **Expert power**—Power that comes from expertise or experience.

✔ **Referral or reference power**—Power derived by sharing or linking needed contacts, information and resources, or by providing or serving as a reference to help someone achieve their objectives.

✔ **Charismatic power**—Power projected from a personality in qualities or characteristics, such as persuasion, articulation, manners, temperament and physical appeal.

✔ **Association power**—Power inferred by association with another powerful, influential person.

Ways to Enhance Your Power

Never underestimate anyone because of his/her position or status. Truly powerful people respect the contribution of every person, regardless of status, position, title or other outward status symbols. They treat each person with gracious courtesy and respect.

Be a person of your word. Let your actions follow your words. Do what you say you will do. Never offer excuses. Return phone calls and answer letters. Share information, resources and contacts. Train, cross-train, make referrals and serve as a reference. Demonstrate irreproachable ethics and integrity. With power comes responsibility. Your actions will be scrutinized. Remember that the only true power is power earned every day, through consistency of actions.

► **Project a consistent, positive, enthusiastic attitude.** Humor, graciousness, etiquette and protocol are qualities essential to garner the support essential to the power figure.

► **Treat the company's time and resources as** if they were from your own personal bank account. To maximize opportunities, creatively and innovatively seek ways to reduce costs and waste. Make the company's issues and goals your own issues and goals.

EXERCISES: IDENTIFY POWERFUL WOMEN

Exercise #1

Identify the one or more types of power which each of the following leaders/ managers project most strongly. If you believe a particular woman possesses more than one type of power, rank the types, with #1 being the strongest. List reasons and examples of how she demonstrates each type of power.

POWERFUL WOMEN			
	Type of Power	**Reason**	**Qualities**
Liz Claiborne			
Ann Richards			
Mary Kay			
Barbara Jordan			
Katherine Graham			
Mother Teresa			
Margaret Thatcher			
Hillary Clinton			
You			

Exercise #2

Identify two women managers or leaders within your company, organization or profession. What types of power do you believe they possess? Give reasons, characteristics and examples.

EXAMPLES   TYPE OF POWER   REASON   QUALITIES

1. _____

2. _____

How could you benefit from knowing or working with them on common projects? _____

What can you learn from them? _____

_____

What qualities do they possess that would be beneficial for you to integrate into your style? _____

TYPES OF MOTIVATION

✔ **Affiliation**—Motivated women tend to be more sensitive to feelings. They value social interactions and relationships with other people. Gregarious, they prefer to work in pairs, groups or teams, focusing on the process or relationships aspects of a project.

✔ **Achievement**—Motivated women are goal-directed, results-oriented, and focus on continuous improvement in their tasks or project accomplishments. Competitive, they attempt to exceed expectations and raise standards. Typically independent, self-directed individuals, they prefer minimal direction, and work best alone, accountable for results. They deserve feedback and recognition for their efforts and accomplishments.

✔ **Power**—Motivated women are typically visionary and conceptual. Power-oriented women thrive on change. They are willing to take necessary risks to lead, to be the first, to try a new approach, to do whatever is necessary to drive a concept or idea to completion. Impatient with rules and procedures that block or impede progress, they will make exceptions; they use their influence to accomplish end results.

Exercise #3

All three motives—affiliation, achievement and power—are important for each individual but one is stronger than the others. Rank your motives from 1 to 3, with 1 being the strongest:

Rank your managers' or associates' motives:

_____ Affiliation   _____ Achievement   _____ Power

Rank one or more of the people closest to you:

Name _____

_____ Affiliation   _____ Achievement   _____ Power

Name _____

_____ Affiliation   _____ Achievement   _____ Power

SEXUAL HARASSMENT

Since women often are the sole supporters of their children, they have to keep their jobs at any cost and are, therefore, often in precarious predicaments. One of the most harrowing ordeals that many women in business face, regardless of marital status or economic position, is sexual harassment. This is difficult, although not impossible to prove. And, as the Anita Hill–Clarence Thomas fiasco showed, the woman who accuses someone of sexual harassment often faces a firestorm.

The Senate confirmation hearings for Clarence Thomas angered women more than any event in recent history. It inspired the highest number of women ever to run for public office; it increased the number of organizations providing sexual-harassment awareness training. And it resulted in updated policies on harassment and discrimination.

What Is Sexual Harassment?

Sexual harassment is deliberate or repeated, unwelcome, uninvited, unreturned or extended advances that create a hostile work environment and makes it difficult for someone to do his or her job. As a result of the 1986 landmark case, *Meritor Savings Bank v. Vinson* and a 1991 law, victims of sexual harassment can now sue for damages between $50,000 and $300,000, depending on the company size.

Sexual harassment should be taken seriously. It is offensive, objectionable behavior that is sexual in nature, creates an implicit or explicit condition for employment, causes discomfort or humiliation, interferes with the recipient's job performance, and/or qualifies as a form of sex discrimination under Title VII, the Civil Rights Act of 1964. Sexual harassment includes, but is not limited to:

1. **Verbal**

   • Dirty jokes, sexually explicit statements, teasing remarks or questions that have sexual overtones.

2. **Subtle pressure for sexual activity**

   • Flirting behavior that implies a promotion or reward for sexual favors, as in preferred job assignments or job security; pressure for dates off the job, for whatever reason.

SEXUAL HARASSMENT (continued)

3. **Rape or attempted rape.**

   - Forced sexual penetration, sexually suggestive looks or gestures.

4. **Coercive pressure for sexual activity**

   - Threats of job loss or other punishment if favors are not granted.

5. **Confrontation**

   - Phone calls or materials of a sexual nature.

Because sexual harassment can lead to feelings of guilt, a tarnished reputation, anxiety and economic losses for the recipient, any form should be taken seriously. Men, as well as women, have reported experiencing sexual harassment. In fact, many victims have sued successfully in court to win civil actions against employers who were guilty of sexual harassment or companies that knowingly allowed the practice to continue. To handle sexual harassment:

► Privately tell the offender to stop the offending action in an assertive, direct manner. For example, "John, touching me makes me uncomfortable. I would like for you to stop."

► Know your company's policy and procedures about sexual harassment.

► Document any incidents and how the behaviors are linked to your employment and/or interfere with your work, in case you need to file a grievance or eventually provide evidence. Detail who was involved, what, where, and when it took place, and possible witnesses.

► Establish a confidant. Confide in a trusted friend. This can provide both support and documentation of your situation.

► Save all correspondence that you send or receive. If you were sent indecent notes—save them.

► Find out if there are other victims. You might find emotional support and be able to combine resources.

► Establish your own support network. Let your family, friends or clergy know what you are going through.

Become a role model in your organization. Help to affect policies that will provide a safe workplace, free from fear of intimidation for all employees.

MANAGING STRESS

> *"The best career advice given to the young is, find out what you like doing best and get someone to pay you for doing it."*
>
> Katherine Whitehorn (1928–   )
> British columnist

If you feel like many women, working harder and enjoying it less, pressured by multiple responsibilities and roles, learning to manage stress is essential not only for a balanced life, but for a successful career.

Stress is a condition of strain on one's emotions, thought processes or physical condition. Stress is not so much the situation, as it is our reaction to the situation. In other words, most of the negative impact associated with stress comes from our negative *reaction* to the stress, rather than the stress itself.

The woman manager faces several sources of stress, such as multiple commitments, work overload or underload, conflicting demands, perfectionism, and balance between family and work. Women do not just give at the office; as we saw earlier, they typically give another fifteen-plus hours a week to household chores that men do not.

Increasingly, women want balance and flexibility. Felice Schwartz, president of Catalyst, proposed the "Mommy Track," in a landmark *Harvard Business Review* article. This concept provides "an alternative career track for working mothers to meet the need for greater flexibility and to attract the best employees and increase productivity."

Having it all is not just career, husband and children. It is relationships, career, balance and leisure time. Stress can be a destructive force, brought on by too much work and not enough play, which can ultimately damage your relationships and your health.

Although stress is a daily part of our lives and is usually expressed in negative terms, it is not inherently bad. A wedding, promotion or graduation can be as stressful as a transfer, layoff or conflicting deadlines.

Many diseases, such as ulcers, heart disease and high blood pressure stem from poor stress management.

MANAGING STRESS (continued)

Stressors are anything real or imagined that cause stress. Stressors we feel may be internal, such as the internal drive to do a better job or to achieve a promotion. Other stress comes externally in the form of a demanding boss or an approaching deadline. External stressors are found more commonly in industrialized nations.

Stress can be a powerful, creative force that can improve your life. In fact, a certain amount of stress may actually help us achieve our goals. Alternatively, it can be a negative obsession that constantly blocks your future.

Whether an event is real or perceived, our reaction can have similar effects. Common signs of stress include:

- Irritability

- Short attention span or boredom

- Inability to cope with routine problems

- Anxiety about money

- Suppressed anger

- Loss of sense of humor

- Changes in eating, sleeping, exercise, drinking or smoking habits

EXERCISE: IDENTIFY PRESSURES AFFECTING YOU

We experience both upward and downward pressures at work, which produce stress. Downward pressure comes from top managers or coaches. Upward pressure may come from other employees or team leaders. Check "✓" the top three signs from the list below that indicate stress to you.

Downward Pressure	Upward Pressure
☐ Unrealistic deadlines	☐ Incompetent employees
☐ Insufficient resources or commitment	☐ Inadequately trained employees
☐ Dead-end job	☐ Low morale
☐ Office politics	☐ Pervasive negative attitudes
☐ Uneven workload distribution	☐ Undependable employees
☐ Favoritism	☐ Personality conflicts
☐ Little support or assistance	☐ Overly ambitious employees

EXERCISE: TYPE A OR TYPE B?

How do you typically react when under stress? Do you show any other signs of stress?

ARE YOU A TYPE A OR TYPE B?

Type A Personality

Individuals are characterized by high standards of achievement and an urgency to attain them. They are especially susceptible to stress. Type A's are ulcer-prone, competitive and overachievers.

Do you:

☐ Try to accomplish too many tasks in too little time?

☐ Try to do two things at once, set short deadlines, high standards and then push to accomplish them?

☐ Eat, work, talk or walk at a fast pace, always in a hurry?

☐ Become obsessed with success/achievement, whether in your career or personal goals, measuring progress in terms of performance and time?

☐ Worry about everything—are you likely to become irritated over trivial matters?

☐ Get anxious, tense or nervous when you have to wait?

☐ Feel guilty when relaxing or waiting—do you work on your days off?

If you answered ''yes'' to five or more of these questions, you may be Type A-oriented.

Type B Personality

Individuals are more passive than active in confrontations. They show more sensitivity to the feelings of others in their dealings. Where the Type A might be a workaholic, the Type B will more likely balance her personal life with her work.

Do you:

☐ Realize time limitations and allow realistic estimates in the time required to complete a job?

☐ Have patience with other people and unexpected interruptions?

☐ Maintain a calm attitude with fewer worries?

☐ Accept, rather than fight, circumstances, and try to make the best of the situation?

☐ Take time to enjoy life?

If you answered "yes" to three or more of these questions, you may be Type B-oriented.

Place an "x" by the point on the plot which best illustrates where you are now. Place a circle by the point where you would like to be.

A |———|———|———|———|———| **B**

THE WORKAHOLIC

The workaholic syndrome is a reaction to on-the-job stress—the psychological, emotional, physical and spiritual exhaustion that results from prolonged negative stress. Obsessive, intense and energetic, the workaholic prefers work to leisure, and can and will work anywhere, at anytime. Most workaholics are Type A, driven personalities. Workaholics blur distinctions between work and pleasure. While extra hours are appropriate for short periods of time, working too many long hours can be detrimental. They may lead to *burnout,* an extreme reaction to stress, ultimately characterized by lack of interest and feelings of worthlessness. Burned-out individuals no longer care as intently about work, relationships and/or activities that once interested them. Personal and family life invariably suffer as more time is invested in work than in building or sustaining relationships.

Lighten Up

As comic pianist Victor Borge said, "Laughter is the shortest distance between two people." Taking yourself too seriously can be hazardous to your health and to your career. A sense of humor is now considered a career asset. For example, when CEOs were recently polled on the qualities that prevented women from getting ahead, a "lack of a sense of humor" was in the top five. Although comediennes such as Elaine Boosler, Lily Tomlin and Roseanne Barr help sensitize audiences to women's roles, and enable us to laugh at ourselves, you do not have to be a comedienne to have a sense of humor. Learning to laugh at yourself and situations can enable you to take greater risks, gain proper perspective and enrich relationships.

Tips For Managing Stress

Stress management is a very important step in staying on top.

Stress Quick Check

Place a "✓" beside each of the following suggestions that would benefit you in managing your stress. Place a "+" beside each suggestion that you presently utilize.

☐ Modify your diet to eliminate caffeine, alcohol and refined sugar.

☐ Exercise two to three times a week for at least thirty minutes each workout.

☐ Develop a support system. If you cannot talk to friends or family about your problems, seek out members of the clergy or counseling services.

☐ Decide what is important, according to your own values, priorities and expectations.

☐ Ask for support or assistance or delegate, at work and at home.

☐ Plan personal, private time as conscientiously as you do your workday.

☐ Take frequent, short vacations.

☐ Share your feelings. Ask for what you want, need or expect.

☐ Lighten up! The ability to use humor appropriately and tastefully may not come naturally for everyone, but it can be developed. Dry, impersonal, humorless people tend to alienate others. When used appropriately, laughter heals, disarms, bonds and builds goodwill.

Bad news—the pressures will always be there.

Good news—our reactions to them CAN change.

Appendixes

- Appendix A: Managers' Needs Inventory
- Appendix B: Glossary
- Appendix C: Suggested Readings/Resources

APPENDIX A: *MANAGERS' NEEDS INVENTORY REVIEW*

Listed below are statements describing the needs of supervisors and/or managers. In the box preceding each, place the number 1, 2, or 3, to indicate the degree to which it applies to you (or to your subordinate if you have been asked to evaluate a subordinate's needs). Extremely important = 1; Fairly important = 2; Not too relevant = 3.

- Ability to set realistic goals and standards, define performance requirements, and develop action plans for achieving and controlling (tracking) performance

- Skill in communicating effectively in face-to-face situations—with subordinates, peers, superiors, customers, etc.

- Ability to conduct selection interviews in a way that produces the information needed to make sound hiring decisions, consistent with company policy and the law

- Skill in balancing daily activities between the demands of the task (production-oriented side) and of the employees (people-oriented side)

- Ability to challenge and motivate subordinates, thereby increasing their job satisfaction and developing a team of "turned on" employees

- Skill in giving on-the-job training and counseling relating to behavior at work

- Ability to appraise performance objectively and to conduct regular, constructive performance reviews that are two-way dialogues

- Sensitivity to games people play and the ability to identify their ego states (parent, adult, child) and to deal with them appropriately (transactional analysis)

- Skill in writing letters, memos and reports that are clear, concise, complete and compelling—writing that gets action

- Ability to manage time (of self and others) effectively by prioritizing, controlling interruptions, measuring cost-effectiveness, investing rather than spending time, etc.

APPENDIX A: *MANAGERS' NEEDS INVENTORY REVIEW* (continued)

☐ Skill in cutting costs through methods improvement, work simplification or reallocation, flow charting, analysis of procedures, etc.

☐ Ability to hold meetings, briefings, conferences that are well organized, crisp, and results oriented

☐ Skill in negotiating and resolving conflict, as it arises, in interpersonal relations

☐ Facility in designing in depth, drawing out what is and is not said, summarizing and clarifying, and organizing the speaker's message so that it can be acted upon

☐ Ability to identify problems, to separate causes from symptoms, to evaluate evidence, to weigh alternatives, and to select and implement appropriate solutions

☐ Skill in applying management-by-objectives at the departmental level, preparing action plans, performance documents, etc.

☐ Ability to make effective presentations and to sell ideas in a persuasive, well-documented manner, to managements, to subordinates, to users

APPENDIX B: *GLOSSARY*

affiliation—Socially acquired motives in which a person desires to work with people, serve on committees and teams, and smooth tensions.

agenda—A meeting outline or an outline of goals or objectives that need to be accomplished. A hidden agenda is the underlying motive for a person's behavior, which may not be readily apparent.

aggressive—Expresses feelings in a dishonest, overbearing, pushy, inappropriate manner that violates the other person's rights.

assertiveness—Communication style; standing up for your rights or needs in honest, direct and appropriate ways that do not violate another person's rights.

authority—Potential to get results.

body language—Messages that result from the combination of gestures and postures.

brainstorming—Compiling a large number of solutions to a given problem, without regard to their effectiveness during the creative process.

burnout—Possible reaction to workaholic syndrome. Prolonged negative stress resulting in psychological, physical, emotional and spiritual exhaustion. The person no longer cares about work, relationships and/or activities that once interested her.

commitment—Process of applying resources to a decision to see it through to its desired outcome.

communication skills—To persuade; to present information clearly and effectively.

Delphi—A noninteractional problem-solving technique. The manager collects and tabulates other people's opinions and feedback to determine the best solution.

excellence—Virtue; valuable quality; to surpass, go beyond the limit; intense effort for superior performance; collective commitment to a common purpose. Desire to be the best, to make a difference, insisting on top quality.

fast track—Career path that includes a series of positions leading to an upper management position in less time than usual.

APPENDIX B: *GLOSSARY* (continued)

glass ceiling—Refers to a transparent barrier or subtle discrimination to women's mobility, coined by Ann Morrison, author of *Breaking Through the Glass Ceiling;* impedes women from moving up to senior management, because they are women.

goal—Desired outcome or planned result; long-term objective.

harassment—Any unwanted behavior, whether verbal or physical, that either creates an implicit or explicit condition for employment, or interferes with an individual's ability to work in an atmosphere free from intimidation.

leadership—Ability to influence, persuade, get ideas accepted, to guide willing followers, and to create a positive team climate.

management—Effective utilization of human and material resources, to achieve the objective of the organization.

mentor—Sponsor who advises, teaches, coaches and shares information, to teach the complexities of business.

mommy track—An alternative career track for working mothers to meet the need for greater flexibility and to attract best employees and increase productivity.

negotiation—The art of persuading or influencing someone else to a certain course of action.

networking—Using personal contacts to achieve a goal or objective; trade-offs to share information, business contacts and support.

nonassertiveness—Suppressing needs or desires, appearing to avoid conflicts in a manner that violates personal rights.

objectives—Steps or activities that lead to your goal; building blocks of goals.

plan—To develop managerial activities, to set objectives and to determine appropriate means of achieving the objectives.

power—To have impact, influence, effect change, making things happen, choose to change. Ability to achieve objectives and get results.

problem—Difference or gap between a current situation and a desired or expected situation; any situation that is ''off target,'' unwanted, or urgent enough to warrant attention, analysis or correction.

stress—Condition of strain on one's emotions, thought processes and/or physical condition.

supervision—A subfunction of control that refers to the overseeing of subordinates' work activity.

visualization—Practice of seeing yourself achieve goals; mental rehearsal to prepare your mind for coming success, to become comfortable with the idea of success.

APPENDIX C: *SUGGESTED READINGS/RESOURCES*

Aburdene, Patricia and John Naisbett. *Megatrends for Women*. Villard Books, NY, NY. 1992.

Aburdene, Patricia and John Naisbett. *Megatrends 2000*. Wm. Morrow & Company, NY, NY. 1990.

Brown Glaser, Connie and Barbara Steinberg Smalley. *More Power To! How Women Communicate Their Way to Success*. Warner Books, NY, NY. 1992.

duPont, M. Kay. *Business Etiquette and Professionalism*. Crisp Publications, Los Altos, CA. 1990.

Haragan, Betty. *Games Mother Never Taught You: Corporate Games for Women*. Warner Books, NY, NY. 1977.

Hardesty, Sarah and Nehana Jacobs. *Success and Betrayal*, Simon and Schuster. NY, NY. 1986.

Leeds, Dorothy. *Smart Questions*. Berkley, NY, NY. 1988.

Lightle, Juliana and Betsy Doucet. *Sexual Harassment in the Workplace*. Crisp Publications, Menlo Park, CA. 1992.

Manning, Marilyn and Patricia Haddock. *Leadership Skills for Women*. Crisp Publications, Los Altos, CA. 1989.

Morrison, Ann. *Breaking the Glass Ceiling*. Addison Wesley, Reading, MA. 1987.

Popcorn, Faith. *The Popcorn Report*. Doubleday Currency, NY, NY. 1991.

Simons, George F., and Deborah Weismann. *Men and Women: Partners at Work*. Crisp Publications, Los Altos, CA. 1990.

Sitterly, Connie. *The Female Entrepreneur*. Crisp Publications, Menlo Park, CA. 1993.

Sitterly, Connie and Beth Duke. *A Woman's Place: Management*. Prentice Hall, Englewood Cliffs, NJ. 1989.

Tannen, Deborah. *You Just Don't Understand: Women and Men in Conversation*. William Morrow & Company, NY, NY. 1991.

NOTES

NOTES

We hope you enjoyed this book. If so, we have good news for you. This title is part of the best-selling *FIFTY-MINUTE*™ *Series* of books. All *Series* books are similar in size and identical in price. Several are supported with training videos (identified by the symbol **V** next to the title).

FIFTY-MINUTE Books and Videos are available from your distributor. A free catalog is available upon request from Crisp Publications, Inc., 1200 Hamilton Court, Menlo Park, California 94025.

FIFTY-MINUTE Series Books & Videos organized by general subject area.

Management Training:

V	Coaching & Counseling	68-8
	Conducting Training Sessions	193-7
	Delegating for Results	008-6
	Developing Instructional Design	076-0
V	Effective Meeting Skills	33-5
V	Empowerment	096-5
	Ethics in Business	69-6
	Goals & Goal Setting	183-X
	Handling the Difficult Employee	179-1
V	An Honest Day's Work: Motivating Employees	39-4
V	Increasing Employee Productivity	10-8
V	Leadership Skills for Women	62-9
	Learning to Lead	43-4
V	Managing Disagreement Constructively	41-6
V	Managing for Commitment	099-X
	Managing the Older Work Force	182-1
V	Managing Organizational Change	80-7
	Managing the Technical Employee	177-5
	Mentoring	123-6
V	The New Supervisor—Revised	120-1
	Personal Performance Contracts—Revised	12-2
V	Project Management	75-0
V	Quality at Work: A Personal Guide to Professional Standards	72-6
	Rate Your Skills As a Manager	101-5
	Recruiting Volunteers: A Guide for Nonprofits	141-4
	Risk Taking	076-9
	Selecting & Working with Consultants	87-4
	Self-Managing Teams	00-0
	Successful Negotiation—Revised	09-2
	Systematic Problem Solving & Decision Making	63-7

Management Training (continued):

(v)	Team Building—Revised	118-X
	Training Managers to Train	43-2
	Training Methods That Work	082-5
	Understanding Organizational Change	71-8
(v)	Working Together in a Multicultural Organization	85-8

Personal Improvement:

(v)	Attitude: Your Most Priceless Possession—Revised	011-6
	Business Etiquette & Professionalism	32-9
	Concentration!	073-6
	The Continuously Improving Self: A Personal Guide to TQM	151-1
(v)	Developing Positive Assertiveness	38-6
	Developing Self-Esteem	66-1
	Finding Your Purpose: A Guide to Personal Fulfillment	072-8
	From Technical Specialist to Supervisor	194-X
	Managing Anger	114-7
	Memory Skills in Business	56-4
	Organizing Your Workspace	125-2
(v)	Personal Time Management	22-X
	Plan Your Work—Work Your Plan!	078-7
	Self-Empowerment	128-7
	Stop Procrastinating: Get to Work!	88-2
	Successful Self-Management	26-2
	The Telephone & Time Management	53-X
	Twelve Steps to Self-Improvement	102-3

Human Resources & Wellness:

	Attacking Absenteeism	042-6
(v)	Balancing Home & Career—Revised	35-3
	Downsizing Without Disaster	081-7
	Effective Performance Appraisals—Revised	11-4
	Effective Recruiting Strategies	127-9
	Employee Benefits with Cost Control	133-3
	Giving & Receiving Criticism	023-X
	Guide to Affirmative Action	54-8
	Guide to OSHA	180-5
	Health Strategies for Working Women	079-5
(v)	High Performance Hiring	088-4
(v)	Job Performance & Chemical Dependency	27-0
(v)	Managing Personal Change	74-2
	Managing Upward: Managing Your Boss	131-7
(v)	Men and Women: Partners at Work	009-4
(v)	Mental Fitness: A Guide to Stress Management	15-7
	New Employee Orientation	46-7
	Office Management: A Guide to Productivity	005-1
	Overcoming Anxiety	29-9
	Personal Counseling	14-9
	Personal Wellness: Achieving Balance for Healthy Living	21-3
	Preventing Job Burnout	23-8

Human Resources & Wellness (continued):

	Productivity at the Workstation: Wellness & Fitness at Your Desk	41-8
	Professional Excellence for Secretaries	52-1
	Quality Interviewing—Revised	13-0
	Sexual Harassment in the Workplace	153-8
	Stress That Motivates: Self-Talk Secrets for Success	150-3
	Wellness in the Workplace	20-5
	Winning at Human Relations	86-6
	Writing a Human Resources Manual	70-X
(v)	Your First Thirty Days in a New Job	003-5

Communications & Creativity:

	The Art of Communicating	45-9
(v)	Writing Business Proposals & Reports—Revised	25-4
(v)	The Business of Listening	34-3
	Business Report Writing	122-8
	Creative Decision Making	098-1
(v)	Creativity in Business	67-X
	Dealing Effectively with the Media	116-3
(v)	Effective Presentation Skills	24-6
	Facilitation Skills	199-6
	Fifty One-Minute Tips to Better Communication	071-X
	Formatting Letters & Memos on the Microcomputer	130-9
	Influencing Others	84-X
(v)	Making Humor Work	61-0
	Speedreading in Business	78-5
	Technical Presentation Skills	55-6
	Technical Writing in the Corporate World	004-3
	Think on Your Feet	117-1
	Visual Aids in Business	77-7
	Writing Fitness	35-1

Customer Service/Sales Training:

	Beyond Customer Service: The Art of Customer Retention	115-5
(v)	Calming Upset Customers	65-3
(v)	Customer Satisfaction—Revised	084-1
	Effective Sales Management	31-0
	Exhibiting at Tradeshows	137-6
	Improving Your Company Image	136-8
	Managing Quality Customer Service	83-1
	Measuring Customer Satisfaction	178-3
	Professional Selling	42-4
(v)	Quality Customer Service—Revised	95-5
	Restaurant Server's Guide—Revised	08-4
	Sales Training Basics—Revised	119-8
	Telemarketing Basics	60-2
(v)	Telephone Courtesy & Customer Service—Revised	064-7

Small Business & Financial Planning:

The Accounting Cycle	146-5
The Basics of Budgeting	134-1
Consulting for Success	006-X
Creative Fund Raising	181-3
Credits & Collections	080-9
Direct Mail Magic	075-2
Financial Analysis: Beyond the Basics	132-5
Financial Planning with Employee Benefits	90-4
Marketing Your Consulting or Professional Services	40-8
Personal Financial Fitness—Revised	89-0
Publicity Power	82-3
Starting Your New Business—Revised	144-9
Understanding Financial Statements	22-1
Writing & Implementing a Marketing Plan	083-3

Adult Literacy & Learning:

Adult Learning Skills	175-9
Basic Business Math	24-8
Becoming an Effective Tutor	28-0
Building Blocks of Business Writing	095-7
Clear Writing	094-9
The College Experience: Your First Thirty Days on Campus	07-8
Easy English	198-8
Going Back to School: An Adult Perspective	142-2
Introduction to Microcomputers: The Least You Should Know	087-6
Language, Customs & Protocol for Foreign Students	097-3
Improve Your Reading	086-8
Returning to Learning: Getting Your G.E.D.	02-7
Study Skills Strategies—Revised	05-X
Vocabulary Improvement	124-4

Career/Retirement & Life Planning:

Career Discovery—Revised	07-6
Developing Strategic Resumes	129-5
Effective Networking	30-2
I Got the Job!—Revised	121-X
Job Search That Works	105-8
Plan B: Protecting Your Career from Change	48-3
Preparing for Your Interview	33-7